WILLIAM SHENSTONE

WILLIAM SHENSTONE

An Eighteenth-Century Portrait

by

A. R. HUMPHREYS

CAMBRIDGE
AT THE UNIVERSITY PRESS
1937

PR
3677
.H8
2009

CAMBRIDGE UNIVERSITY PRESS
Cambridge, New York, Melbourne, Madrid, Cape Town, Singapore,
São Paulo, Delhi, Dubai, Tokyo

Cambridge University Press
The Edinburgh Building, Cambridge CB2 8RU, UK

Published in the United States of America by Cambridge University Press, New York

www.cambridge.org
Information on this title: www.cambridge.org/9780521125277

First published 1937
This digitally printed version 2009

A catalogue record for this publication is available from the British Library

ISBN 978-0-521-05349-5 Hardback
ISBN 978-0-521-12527-7 Paperback

To

MY FATHER AND MOTHER

CONTENTS

PREFACE

The following pages are a slight offshoot of work on the eighteenth century which I undertook while enjoying the hospitality of Harvard University and the munificence of a Commonwealth Fund Fellowship. To the Commonwealth Fund and its administrators in England and America I feel a deeper debt of gratitude than I can put into words. The opportunities afforded for lasting friendships, and for experiences ranging far beyond the academic, could be deserved only by the most meritorious of mortals; others, like myself, conscious of no such deserts, can only marvel that good fortune should visit them so richly. To Professor C. N. Greenough, of Harvard University, who supervised this book in its embryo form with the most kindly encouragement, it is a pleasure to express my gratitude. In England I have been greatly helped by the general criticisms of Mr T. R. Henn, Dr A. D. M. Hoare, Mr L. F. Powell, Mr S. C. Roberts, and Miss Marjorie Williams; Mr Robert Gardner-Medwin and Mr Denis Winston will, I hope, recognize in Part II the improvements they suggested, and accept my deep thanks for them; while to the kindness of Mrs E. Stevenson, the present lessee of The Leasowes, I owe my brief but illuminating exploration of Shenstone's estate.

A. R. H.

September 1937

PART I

A FUGITIVE AND CLOISTERED VIRTUE

Baiana nostri villa, Basse, Faustini
non otiosis ordinata myrtetis,
viduaque platano, tonsilique buxeto,
ingrata lati spatia detinet campi;
sed rure vero barbaroque lætatur.

MARTIAL

It is easy to enjoy the oases which the eighteenth century offers, and to overlook their significance as symbols of cultural order. The century had its worries, and thought them serious; but compared with the convulsions of other generations they dwindle to eddies in an even stream. The fugitive and cloistered virtue, sedulously sheltered from the alarms of conflict, found many refuges in England from the time of Sir Roger de Coverley to that of Catherine Morland; it was able to develop appropriately and benignly.

Yet as the literary historian pursues his search for 'influences' and 'origins'—those elusive abstractions —he sometimes loses sight of this placid normality. The dynamic, the evolutionary, gestures of history and literature fascinate the eye. The lines of generalization which are the goal of all who impose pattern on the past demand movement; the interdependence of generations must be established, the change of tone defined. And this in many ways is right and proper; we can see that many important ideas of the Romantic Revival, naturalism, religious earnestness, humanitarian sentiment, and social disintegration, are deeply rooted in the eighteenth century. Nevertheless, the desire to see history as a continuum need not confuse the characters of successive generations. The mellow knowledge of Austin Dobson, and the wisdom of Saintsbury, surveying eighteenth-century literature as 'a place of rest and refreshment', may counterbalance our eagerness to trace the dynamism of ideas. It is salutary from time to time to remember the large part of the century which did not run for immortal garlands, which did not sally out to seek its adversaries, which decorously avoided the dust and heat of the day, and retired to retreats where the tide of life flowed in a sequence only varied by the accidents of mortality and the rhythm of the seasons. In such a retreat, Timothy the tortoise could peer wisely over the edge of Gilbert White's ha-ha, and leave his reverend master wondering at his sagacity; the country parson could exchange with surprising ease the social liveliness of a university for the somnolent repetitions of a country cure; wars and rumours of wars could penetrate only with a remote reverberation; a journey to London could last a week or more; country folk, as Thomas Holcroft describes them at the end of the century, could meet to sing Purcell, Croft, Greene, Boyce and Handel; descendant was gathered to ancestor in the same grave; and human life might, if it so willed, approach wonderfully near the placidity of a vegetable.

It is important to remember how much of England lived far from the ignoble strife of crowds. The magnetism of London for literary men and place-seekers, Johnson's belief that it was the most concentrated focus of genius in Europe, and its natural preponderance in record, have enabled it to dominate cultural history. From Addison onward through Hogarth to Johnson it has appeared the embodiment of the eighteenth century, while Johnson himself seems in many ways to contain London in the very bones of his large and awkward frame. He focuses attention on himself so that for the *Cambridge History of English Literature* his generation is the 'Age of Johnson'; and what he himself does not supply of London society, from the time when he walked the streets with Richard Savage, may largely be provided by Horace Walpole. In the London of to-day the observer can most readily sense how remote he is from the world which produced the austere dignity of Georgian architecture and the elegances of the Adam brothers. But London, even with Johnson and Walpole, is not all the eighteenth century; the focal attraction of the capital has given to city life an importance which needs to be qualified.

As the century advanced, there was a certain decentralization of culture, as the centre and circumference grew to know more about each other. The main cause for this was the improvement in transport. Conservatives, it is true, sometimes lamented the extension of good roads, as a drain on the country and a debasement of rural simplicity. John Byng, Viscount Torrington, deplored 'the baneful luxury of turnpikes', and declared: 'I wish with all my heart that half the turnpike roads of the kingdom were ploughed up, which have imported London manners and depopulated the country—I meet milkmaids out on the roads with the dress and looks of Strand misses, and must think that every line of Goldsmith's *Deserted Village* contains melancholy truths.' Even Arthur Young, who preferred good turnpikes to bad cart-tracks, was worried by the drain on the rural population which followed the introduction of cheap and speedy travel. But the countryside was correspondingly enlivened. During one month in 1770, Woodforde sees *The Beggar's Opera, Hamlet, Richard III, Chrononhotontologos*, and various other entertainments, in his Somerset village of Castlecary. James Lackington, a bookseller of London, who wrote his *Memoirs* and published them in 1791, remarks how 'more than four times the number of books are sold now than were sold twenty years since. The poorer sort of farmers, and even the poor country people in general, who before that period spent their winter evenings in relating stories of witches, ghosts, hobgoblins, &c., now shorten the winter nights by hearing their sons and daughters read tales, romances, &c. and on entering their houses, you may see *Tom Jones, Roderick Random*, and other entertaining books stuck up on their bacon racks, &c. If

John goes to town with a load of hay, he is charged to be sure not to forget to bring home *Peregrine Pickle's adventures*; and when *Dolly* is sent to market to sell her eggs, she is commissioned to purchase *The history of Pamela Andrews*.' 'In short', declares Lackington, 'all ranks and degrees now R E A D.' Such devotees of literature were clearly far more sophisticated people than the outmoded ladies at Court in 1742, as Walpole describes them, 'in all the accoutrements that were in use in Queen Anne's days', or than the country gentleman like Squire Western, who was, according to Shenstone, 'a natural picture of thousands of His Majesty's rural subjects'. Lackington's *Memoirs* deserve to be better known, both for their general cheerfulness and for their information on the century's reading. A study of rural culture about 1750 may illuminate literary and artistic movements away from the capital, at that hesitant time when literature and taste, halting between two worlds, had to meditate their way into a new fruition.

Saintsbury and W. H. Hutton, in the *Cambridge History*, and various historians of pre-Romanticism in humbler works, have hinted at the liberating influence of Shenstone and his circle of friends. The full edition of his letters promised by Marjorie Williams should do a great deal in revealing an attractive, reflective mind with many interests and excitements. It would be unwise to claim for Shenstone, or for his friends (except Thomas Percy), a decisive influence on any artistic or poetic movement, yet the homage so frequently paid to him by his contemporaries and immediate successors was paid to one who developed an individual, though spiritually inadequate, way of life, who cultivated a personal sensibility, who illuminated in his verse, letters, and *pensées* a Virgilian rusticity which was near to the heart of the eighteenth century, with its gentleman farmers and literate aristocracy. To apply to social history in general a pattern evolved from a single one of its many aspects would be misleading. But in that leisurely, well-mannered group of friends who circulated round Shenstone's elegant estate, the current of whose life flowed peacefully in some of England's loveliest landscapes, we can feel country society at its best, because it is unsophisticated by a conscious pose. Quietly social, mildly literary, it flowers into a faint completeness of spirit, and lives within the bounds of an unconscious decorum.

.   .   .   .   .   .

William Shenstone was born on 18 November 1714, at Halesowen, an outlying part of Shropshire, and was baptized in the church there on 6 December. In this place his ancestors had been established at least since 1575, for at that date the name appears on the parish registers. At any rate, whatever the family's previous history, his father and grandfather had been farmers in the parish, the latter purchasing the farm of The Leasowes, which the poet's gardening abilities were to make the goal of sociable pilgrimage. His father, Thomas Shenstone, inherited the estate, and married Anne Penn, one of the daughters of William

Penn of Harborough; their only children were William and his brother Joseph, who was trained as an attorney at Bridgnorth but never practised, and whose death in 1751 was one of the severest afflictions of the poet's career.

From his birth he was submitted to the natural beauties of a delightfully pastoral country, which, as he declares in the essay prefixed to his elegies, provided the truest and most delicate imagery of his poetry. 'If he describes a rural landskip', he wrote of himself, 'or unfolds the train of sentiments it inspired, he fairly drew his picture from the spot; and felt very sensibly the affection he communicates. If he speaks of his humble shed, his flocks and his fleeces, he does not counterfeit the scene; who having (whether through choice or necessity is not material) retired betimes to country solitudes, and sought his happiness in rural employments, has a right to consider himself as a real shepherd. The flocks, the meadows, and the grottos, are *his own*, and the embellishment of his *farm* his sole amusement.' And very early he showed a love for reading which, it is recorded, engrossed him so much that, if his parents forgot to purchase books at the country fairs they attended, his mother had to disguise a block of wood and carry it up to him in bed, to induce him, by this simple deception, to go to sleep, if not to awaken, in a state of contentment.

The third determining influence in his life was ill health. For the cause of this Havelock Ellis, prefacing a selection of the *pensées* which Shenstone grouped together and called *Men and Manners*, suggested premature birth. It is probable, however, that a constitutional weakness affected all his family, for his father died in 1724, his mother just before he went to Oxford in 1732, and his brother before reaching the age of thirty. Shenstone himself died, or rather ceased to live, in his forty-ninth year, after a life in which the ills of age set in before youth was properly over. He describes himself, in 1741, as 'habitually dispirited', and the tone of humorous exaggeration in which he often recounts his woes does not conceal a continual struggle with illness. An *Ode to Health* bears the date 1730, when he was only sixteen, but this can hardly be correct, as its tone is mature, its style developed, and it mentions

> my well-known grove,
> Where mineral fountains vainly bear
> Thy boasted name and titles fair.

This is presumably a reference to the chalybeate spring at The Leasowes, the dedication of which—

> Fons ferrugineus
> Divae quae secessu isto
> Frui concedit
> Saluti S.—

is discussed in letters between 1751 and 1753. But whatever the date of the poem, its subject-matter faithfully reflects Shenstone's situation.

> O Health, capricious maid!
> Why dost thou shun my peaceful bow'r,
> Where I had hope to share thy pow'r,
> And bless thy lasting aid?

Since thou, alas! art flown,
It 'vails not whether muse or grace,
With tempting smile, frequent the place;
I sigh for thee alone.

Age not forbids thy stay;
Thou yet might'st act the friendly part;
Thou yet might'st raise this languid heart;
Why speed so swift away?

     *   *   *

There was, there was a time,
When tho' I scorn'd thy guardian care,
Nor made a vow, nor said a pray'r,
I did not rue the crime.

Who then more blest than I?
When the glad school-boy's task was done,
And forth, with jocund sprite, I run
To freedom, and to joy?

How jovial then the day!
What since have all my labours found,
Thus climbing life, to gaze around,
That can thy loss repay?

This despondency is never in Shenstone an affectation. It permeates the letters and many of the poems with a sad persistence, though the letters also record many moods of lively humour and excited interest. The drawbacks of a weak constitution begin to overshadow his life at an early age; it is sufficient to notice how much of an individual reaction his melancholy was, how little it depended on a fashionable cult. His state of mind could frequently, especially in winter, be summarized as the *Oxford Dictionary* defines melancholia—'a functional mental disease characterized by gloomy thoughtfulness, ill-grounded fears, and general depression of mind.' Shenstone at times suffered from these symptoms, but he had them as a personal dower, and drew no auto-suggestive gloom from a romantic addiction to disease.

The resulting indolence of body worried him, disturbed his friends, and made it difficult for those of a livelier disposition to sympathize. It invalidated, but did not soothe, his mind. He wrote an *Ode to Indolence*, desiring that the soul tied to such an inactive frame should cease from its uneasiness and find the same salvation that the body finds in rest. The attitude of unsympathetic circles was, as a result, one of pitying contempt. 'Poor Shenstone!' was the almost invariable comment of Walpole. Gray's deeper nature held the same opinion, with more sincerity but still rather unfairly: 'Poor Man! he was always wishing for money, for fame, & other distinctions, & his whole philosophy consisted in living against his will in retirement, & in a place wch his taste had adorn'd; but wch he only enjoy'd when People of note came to see & commend it.' Such opinions would, I think, have been partly revised had the letters printed in his collected works in 1769 included the cheerful ones written to his friend Lady Luxborough. Johnson's *Life* is an unconvincing attempt not to be hostile. The Doctor himself, sometimes so languid that he could not distinguish the hour upon the town clock, affected with a kind of St Vitus's dance, half-blind from scrofula, and from time to time, in the words of Boswell, 'overwhelmed

with an horrible hypochondria, with perpetual irrita-
tion, fretfulness, and impatience', had won his way
by sheer energy of brain, endeavouring to prove that,
where dictionaries were concerned, one Englishman
in three years could equal the achievement of forty
Frenchmen in forty years. The vicissitudes of his
mental distress were more violent than those which
Shenstone had to support, but he could not understand a man who retreated under the attack of
depression, and he treated with scorn the arguments
of temperamental creatures like Gray, who maintained that poetry was a matter of moods. Even
Shenstone's friends were baffled. Robert Dodsley,
who performed one of the last offices of friendship by
collecting together and introducing his works, believed that 'he had a sublimity equal to the highest
attempts; yet from the indolence of his temper, he
chose rather to amuse himself in culling flowers at the
foot of the mount, than to take the trouble of climbing the more arduous steeps of Parnassus.' Judging
from the fate of those contemporary poets who tried
to scale the heights of the mountain, we need not
lament Shenstone's modesty. But other friends also
found his indolence puzzling. Richard Graves, the
lively author of that jovial novel *The Spiritual
Quixote*, was his nearest companion from his Oxford
days, and was so disturbed by his lack of energy that
he wrote another novel, *Columella; or, The Distressed
Anchoret*. This work, while it was published sixteen
years after Shenstone's death and does not at all
points resemble his plight, yet clearly draws its moral

[11]

against seclusion from the example of The Leasowes. 'The principal subject of the following narrative', says Graves, 'is a real fact.' It is the tale of a young man who, 'after having been prepared by a liberal education, and a long and regular course of studies, for some learned or ingenious profession,... retires in the vigour of life through mere indolence and love of ease, and spends his days in solitude and inactivity', and thereby 'not only robs the community of an useful member in a more elevated sphere, but probably lays the foundation of his own infelicity.'

Yet, wherever the blame lay, whether in constitutional frailty or mental disposition, there was a compensation. Shenstone's life, almost without his will, grew to a pattern which did not violate the delicate rectitude of his inspiration. However completely he accepted his inheritance, mental, physical, and financial, however weak a will that acceptance denoted, he was enabled to preserve intact the individual promptings of a sensitive nature. Birth into a farming community, rooted in the same soil for a hundred years and more, a childhood environment which did not thwart or sophisticate the simplicity of this inheritance—these things meant a good deal in Shenstone's career. He had, in fact, very little to unlearn.

His father, Dodsley records, was 'a plain uneducated country gentleman... who farmed his own estate', and who, 'sensible of his son's extraordinary capacity, resolved to give him a learned education', and so prepared him for Oxford. His capacity for intimate friendship received its first cultivation when he met Richard Jago, future clergyman and poet, who was destined later to have his best verse, *The Blackbirds*, first attributed to Gilbert West, and then claimed, when it appeared in Dodsley's *Collection of Poems by Several Hands*, by the manager of a theatre in Bath, whose impudence went so far as to assert that 'Jago' was his own pseudonym taken from *Othello*. Jago, born in 1715, was descended from a Cornish family, and his father—likewise named Richard—was the rector of Beaudesert in Warwickshire. Shenstone and he met at the dame school at Halesowen conducted by a certain Sarah Lloyd, in a house which, as Shenstone wrote in 1742, 'is to be seen as thou travellest towards the native home of thy faithful servant.—But she sleeps with her fathers; and is buried with her fathers;—and Thomas her son *reigneth* in her stead!' Despite this eventual fate, however, she rose above sublunary transience sufficiently to inspire her most notable pupil to his best and most delicious poem, *The Schoolmistress*, which felicitously recaptures the old lady's demeanour and aspect:

> Her cap, far whiter than the driven snow,
> Emblem right meet of decency does yield:
> Her apron dy'd in grain, as blue, I trowe,
> As is the hare-bell that adorns the field:
> And in her hand, for scepter, she does wield
> Tway birchen sprays; with anxious fear entwin'd,
> With dark distrust, and sad repentance fill'd;
> And stedfast hate, and sharp affliction join'd,
> And fury uncontroul'd, and chastisement unkind.

[13]

A russet stole was o'er her shoulders thrown;
A russet kirtle fenc'd the nipping air;
'Twas simple russet, but it was her own;
'Twas her own country bred the flock so fair;
'Twas her own labour did the fleece prepare;
And, sooth to say, her pupils, rang'd around,
Thro' pious awe, did term it passing rare;
For they in gaping wonderment abound,
And think, no doubt, she been the greatest wight on
    ground.

Albeit ne flatt'ry did corrupt her truth,
Ne pompous title did debauch her ear;
Goody, good-woman, gossip, n'aunt, forsooth,
Or dame, the sole additions she did hear;
Yet these she challeng'd, these she held right dear:
Ne would esteem him act as mought behove,
Who should not honour'd eld with these revere:
For never title yet so mean could prove,
But there was eke a mind which did that title love.

From the care of Sarah Lloyd Shenstone and Jago
proceeded, as the latter related:

With throbbing heart to the stern discipline
Of pedagogue morose—

that is, of a clergyman named Crumpton who kept an
academy at Solihull, near Birmingham. This gentleman, according to Nash, the historian of Worcestershire, 'had the tuition of many children, sons of the
neighbouring nobility and gentry'. It is ironic that
Jago should particularize his testiness, for Samuel
Johnson once applied for the mastership of the school,

and was rejected because of a report that he was 'a very haughty, ill-natured gent'. Richard Graves, not having suffered from Crumpton's despotism, goes so far in compliment as to say that he 'seems to have given his pupils a more early taste for the English Classics, than was commonly done in grammar schools at that time'. And then Shenstone advanced to Oxford, becoming in 1732 a member of Pembroke College where, just fifty years later, his room was pointed out by Johnson to Hannah More. He matriculated on 25 May.

That famous 'nest of singing birds' had lost Johnson rather more than two years before. But about the time that Shenstone joined it there arrived also Richard Graves and George Whitefield, while Jago went to University College as a servitor. Anthony Whistler, who became a close friend, was admitted at Pembroke in October of the same year. After the death of his mother, Shenstone passed with his brother under the care of an uncle, the Reverend Thomas Dolman, rector of Broome, near Kidderminster, and the family estate was rented and occupied by a distant relation, John Shenstone of Perry Hill in Halesowen parish, until its owner was ready to return to it.

Graves, in that *Recollection of some Particulars in the life of William Shenstone*, which he wrote in 1788 to commemorate his friendship, has described his Oxford career and his companionship with Shenstone with a typical liveliness. He relates how, coming to the university already 'a tolerably good Grecian', he found himself introduced to 'a very sober little party, who amused themselves in the evening with reading Greek and drinking water'. But there were obvious disadvantages about a life of this sort, and he deserted it for 'a set of jolly, sprightly young fellows, most of them west-country lads; who drank ale, smoked tobacco, punned, and sung bacchanalian catches the whole evening'. He next graduated to a group of wine-bibbing, toast-drinking bucks, whose reputation for conviviality no doubt exceeded their real attractions, and he finished the circle of the college's social opportunities in a group of 'plain, sensible, matter-of-fact men, confined to no club, but associating occasionally with each party', whose interests were the law and politics. In each of these groups—except the water-drinkers—Graves encountered Shenstone. It was perhaps the currency of Greek as well as that of water which excluded the poet from the classical abstainers, for he shows no extensive acquaintance with that language. And about this time he was celebrating the attractions of Bacchus in an *Anacreontick* which begins

> Since it is decreed by Fate,
> Friends must sever, soon or late;
> Darkling to their Lodgings roam;
> Stagger to their longest Home;
> Of all Deities the best,
> *Bacchus!* hear a Son's Request!
>
> Let me metamorphos'd be
> Into some wide-spreading Tree:

> In some pleasant flow'ry Glade,
> With my Branches form a Shade.
> Lovers there may bless my Boughs;
> Topers, merrily carouze.

There were, evidently, the germs of camaraderie in the future 'recluse'. Dodsley asserted that 'when young...he was accounted a BEAU', and at least on vacations he caused subdued commotions in the hearts of young ladies.

But traces of his isolation begin to emerge. In the first place, he suffered some embarrassment on account of an ungainly figure—'largely and rather inelegantly formed'—while, says Dodsley, 'his face seemed plain till you conversed with him, and then it grew very pleasing'. He was at times able to be facetious about his awkwardness; a letter written in 1742 relates how, while he was walking in the Mall, the Duke (of Cumberland?) stopped watching a couple of frolicsome dogs in order to stare—'enormously'—at him. Shenstone probably did not attribute to royal families—at least, not to that with which England was blessed at the time—a nice taste in literary matters, and assumed that the Duke's attentions resulted from 'the same [reason] which made him admire the *other* puppy-dogs, because they were large ones'. Later in life he hopes that his portrait-painter will 'lessen my dimensions'. The disability of unwieldiness was not diminished by any Chesterfieldian graces, for, while those move easiest who have learned to dance, Shenstone did not acquire that accomplishment as a youth, and expressed a great contempt for it. Graves attributes his stiffness to his sense that his upbringing had been rustic and limited. 'He used to say', declares Graves, that dancing 'was allowable only in savages, and that in the rudest style, of jumping about, as an expression of joy. But for a set of people, capable of conversing rationally, to start up with an affectation of mirth, which they do not feel, and with *regulated* motions prance about the room, he said, it was like running mad by rule.' Graves might have pointed out to his friend that for running mad by rule there was Terentian precept—surely authority enough for an eighteenth-century gentleman. Shenstone, however, making one of his few approaches to intransigence, and naïvely rationalizing his sense of inferiority, would probably have refused to listen.

The instance itself is trivial, but as a symbol it is significant. Shenstone was one of nature's wallflowers. And one who sat out of the social dance of the eighteenth century, to whom its minuets and gavottes and country dances seemed an unpardonable prancing, more foolish than the rude jumpings of savages, would have to expect a certain misunderstanding, especially from natures like that of Horace Walpole. Graves believes that Shenstone was temperamentally disabled from such lively diversions —'the truth is, there are some persons whom nature has marked with such an air of seriousness and solemnity, that those gaieties, which are very amiable in younger people of a more sprightly appearance, seem quite inconsistent with those more dignified

[18]

characters; and I could as easily reconcile it to my ideas of propriety, to see a chief justice, or an archbishop, display their activity in a cotillon, as to have seen Mr Shenstone footing it in a country dance.' An archbishop might cause amusement in such Gilbertian circumstances; but the embarrassment of Mr Shenstone could only have been painful.

At any rate, he refused to obey conventions which displeased him. The peruke-makers in 1765 were to complain to George III that the gentlemen of London, by wearing their own hair, were precipitating a crisis. Shenstone, however, thirty years before, had adopted the same fashion. His hair, which turned grey very early, was left unconcealed, not, Dodsley assures us, from a desire to be peculiar, but in accordance with a belief that 'every one should dress in a manner most suitable to his own person and figure'. This mild gesture produced a tempered mockery which further isolated him. And though Graves kept meeting him in one college group after another, he never made any intimate friends at Pembroke except Graves himself and Anthony Whistler, a young man who had acquired at Eton an insuperable distaste for languages, along with a slender cultivation of the Muse and a reputedly fine judgment of the Classics—in translation. With these two Shenstone formed a triumvirate to which he referred, on the occasion of Whistler's death in 1754, as 'the greatest happiness, and the greatest pride, of my life'. In addition to these friends there was Jago, but he had few other acquaintances at the university. 'A degree of bashfulness, from his confined education', Graves wrote, 'joined with a consciousness of his own real abilities, made him not inclined to make advances to strangers; indeed, though those that knew him highly loved and esteemed him; yet the singularity of his appearance rather prejudiced some people against him.' Shenstone was throughout his life very selective in his friendships, very dependent on human intimacy and sympathy, and very averse from promiscuous society. His lack of social ease developed a defensive individualism; his timidity rendered the presence and encouragement of his friends essential.

According to Dodsley, his father intended him for the Church: according to Graves he himself meant to become a physician. But neither of these prospects had much to do with his Oxford career, if Graves's story in *Columella* reflects at all accurately the interests of the triumvirate. The three friends, Atticus, Hortensius, and Columella—who undoubtedly represents Shenstone and was recognized as a portrait during Graves's lifetime—spend their time walking and talking together, 'reading some modern poem, a play, or a paper in the *Spectator*, . . . or in very sober and philosophical compotations'. And Columella, instead of applying himself consistently like his friends, turns to the more enchanting regions of poetry and romance, and then retires to a small hereditary estate.

Whether diligent or not, the real-life Columella wrote in 1733 a mock-heroic poem called *The Diamond*, which did not survive for inclusion in the collected works, and a few other poems which did. In 1737 he circulated privately a volume, published anonymously, and modestly entitled, *Poems upon Various Occasions. Written for the Entertainment of the Author, and Printed for the Amusement Of a few Friends Prejudic'd in his Favour.* It bore an appropriate motto from Horace: 'Contentus paucis Lectoribus'. The only poem of note, among these conventional odes and boudoir compliments to a certain 'fair Selinda', is the first version of *The Schoolmistress*, consisting of a mere twelve stanzas.

If at first he was really intended for the Church, he must soon have found his total lack of theological opinions a serious inconvenience. This remained with him throughout his life, 'tho' he had', says Dodsley, 'the most aweful notions of the wisdom, power, and goodness of God'. He soon supplemented this non-committal coolness by an indifference to the vagaries of party politics. Though he supported the interest of George Lyttelton in 1741—'with great warmth', Johnson asserts—when that gentleman unsuccessfully contested Worcestershire, he generally preferred not to participate in the public conflicts of party strife. Graves claims for him considerable powers of political judgment, but the references in his letters, whatever his conversation may have been like, go little further than a balanced common sense, and even so are only infrequent in comparison with most of the other letter-writers of the century. His *Prefatory Essay on Elegy* distinguishes Epic and Tragedy on the one hand from Elegy on the other, as embodying the public virtues as opposed to the private. 'There is a truly virtuous pleasure connected with many pensive contemplations, which it is the province and excellency of elegy to enforce.' For him, life lay always in the elegiac direction, and in the public virtues even his friends had to admit that he was sadly deficient, while.as Johnson remarked, just hinting a fault and hesitating dislike, the 'sullen and surly speculator' might think his performances 'rather the sport than the business of human reason'. In these circumstances Providence, half-kind, presented him with his inheritance. Through the deaths of his mother and of a maternal uncle he came into the possession of The Leasowes and £300 a year, derived from a moiety of the estate at Harborough. He came of age in 1735, and paid a visit to his property during the summer vacation of 1736. Its charms compared so well with those of Oxford, that when term came round he 'prolonged his stay in the country beyond what the business of the college regularly admitted', and though keeping his name on the college books gave up the idea of returning for a degree. In this curiously negative way his lot was determined. Henceforth, the *res angusta domi* joined ill health and indolence as the principal anxieties of his life.

The estate was occupied by a branch of the Shenstone family who were his tenants; and at first the poet boarded with them. He wrote to Graves, in July 1743, describing it in its undeveloped state as 'over-run with shrubs, thickets, and coppices, variegated with barren rocks and precipices, or floated three parts in four with lakes and marshes'. Four years later Horace Walpole, destined to outshine him in the world's eye, went to Strawberry Hill and bought another farm, 'the prettiest bauble you ever saw', set in enamelled meadows with filigree hedges, and thereafter devoted most of his attention to filling it full of suits of armour, rich glass, lean windows adorned with painted saints, taper columns, and wallpaper decorated in perspective to represent 'Gothic' fretwork. Somehow the playfulness of Twickenham Gothic, delicately elegant as it is, looks more unreal after one is acquainted with The Leasowes than it did before, though both estates shared to an important degree that characteristic which gives to eighteenth-century Gothic and naturalism its particular flavour—that is, the imposition of etiquette. The Leasowes will be considered a little later for its development and its relation to taste in general; but at this first introduction it is interesting to note how Shenstone attempted to educate his Arcadia into that proper decorum which even Nature should observe. 'I have', he tells Jago in 1743 or 1744, 'an alcove, six elegies, a seat, two epitaphs (one upon myself), three ballads, four songs, and a serpentine river, to shew you when you come.' And writing to Graves in 1747, in anticipation of a visit from George Lyttelton and James Thomson, he fears that they 'will lavish all their praises upon *nature*, reserving none for poor *art* and *me*'. The pleasant air of important triviality which recalls

Cowper, the intimate relation of poetic and horticultural inspiration, and above all the union of artificiality with the natural, make The Leasowes a symbol of their country and time. Nothing could be further from the turbulent emotion of Rousseau's nature-worship—one might put beside Shenstone's playfulness the following passage from the *Confessions*: 'Jamais pays de plaine, quelque beau qu'il fût, ne parut tel à mes yeux. Il me faut des torrens, des rochers, des sapins, des bois noirs, des montagnes, des chemins raboteux à monter et à descendre, des précipices à mes côtés qui me fassent bien peur.' Shenstone's torrents, rocks, and precipices are altogether less alarming. That there was the element of the turbulent in the pre-Romanticism of England cannot be denied; but much more true to the nature of the eighteenth century was the pleasant, agricultural appreciation, devoid of mystery, of 'the perfection of the shire horse and the mastiff, of the beanfield, the flower-garden, and the great estate, of the avenue of limes and the beeches that crown the hill, of the village green and the heath that refreshes the immense town' (Blunden, *Nature in English Literature*). Somewhere between this hearty realism and the *frisson d'horreur* of Rousseau lies a genre appropriate to the English-Roman age. Shenstone discusses 'the Necessity of smoothing or brushing the Robe of Nature' with Lady Luxborough, whose proposal to fill her lime-walk with shrubs he entirely approves, and whom he is continually advising on the placing of an urn, the planting of a shrubbery, or the geography of a terrace, 'in order to maintain a due Proportion betwixt the Objects you introduce; that you may not have so much *Lawn*, as to have none of the Beauty of *Plantations*; so much *Wood* as to have no *Flower-work*, & so on.' At a later stage of the naturalistic movement any traces of human handiwork were likely to arouse contempt, as they did in Uvedale Price, that devoted theorist whose *Essay on the Picturesque as compared with the Sublime and the Beautiful* appeared in 1794–8. But Shenstone represents the transitional period when, though the hand of art was not supposed to tamper with nature —at any rate 'other than clandestinely and by night' as he observed—it did so very extensively and clearly, and left its urns here and its alcoves there. But then, he wrote, 'apparent art, in its proper province, is almost as important as apparent nature. They contrast agreeably; but their provinces ever should be kept distinct.' It was a Horatian ideal of landscape, where a well-groomed nature, existing for man's alleviation, enshrined in its nooks and amphitheatres memories which added to natural beauty the pleasing overtones of melancholy.

This retreat, accepted by the poet in a completely raw and unimproved state, provided in its cultivation all the entertainment which his sensitive but frail nature demanded, apart from the amusement of exchanging poems and criticisms with his friends, and of paying occasional visits to London, Worcester, or elsewhere. It attracted to him a stream of friendly visitors, and within its little benevolent despotism provided an exercise for his creative ability which the stress of town life would probably have subdued. As Horace asked in that ode to simplicity which, like Shenstone, spurned the uninitiate crowd:

> Cur invidendis postibus et novo
> Sublime ritu moliar atrium?
> Cur valle permutem Sabina
> Divitias operosiores?

Shenstone's retirement differed from that of Horace in that it was less a matter of theory than one of fact, and also in that all his life he desired a fuller share than he could obtain of those riches which the Roman poet assures us are so oppressive.

He did not start to beautify his grounds immediately he left Oxford. At first he resided partly at Harborough, and partly at The Leasowes, where Graves visited him to pass the time in pleasant conversation and desultory reading. He wrote to Graves later with affection of these 'Days of Fancy and dear Enthusiasm', 'when the *merum Rus* of the *Leasowes* could furnish you with pleasanter Ideas, than the noblest Scenes that ever Painter copied'. Not far away, at Snitterfield in Warwickshire, where Shakespeare's father and grandfather had owned property, Jago had held his curacy since 1737, and through him Shenstone came to know Henrietta, Lady Luxborough, with whom he was to correspond briskly for several years. Of these friends Graves was the liveliest. Born in 1715, he passed from Abingdon Grammar School to Pembroke College in 1732, and took his degree in 1736 on the same day as George Whitefield. He was elected a Fellow of All Souls, and studied medicine in London, but after a severe attack of nervous fever returned to Oxford to enter the ministry. He was ordained in 1740 and presented to the living of Tissington in Derbyshire. Here he remained for four years; then, obtaining a curacy at Aldworth, near Reading, he resided with a gentleman farmer named Bartholomew. Mr Bartholomew had a daughter Lucy, and Graves, with a curious mixture of rashness and common sense, married her in 1747 when she was only sixteen, and the next year sent her to London for an education. The experiment, despite the head-shakings of his friends, was a complete success. From 1748 until his death in 1804 Graves held the rectorship of Claverton, near Bath, where he earned the friendship of Ralph Allen and his family at Prior Park, and of Bishop Warburton, whose only son he educated. He was short and slight in build, with features of a humorous and quizzical sharpness; he gained an acquaintance with nearly all the *beau monde* who frequented Bath, and amused them by the liveliness with which he walked into the town almost every day, until the year of his death. His main literary monument was his full-blooded satire on Methodism, *The Spiritual Quixote, or the Summer's Ramble of Mr Geoffry Wildgoose*. He was attended during his last illness by Malthus the political economist, who had once been his pupil.

Of Jago, John Scott Hylton, a later friend of

Shenstone's, left a portrait when he edited his poems in 1784: 'Mr Jago, in his person, was about the middle stature. In his manner, like most people of sensibility, he appeared reserved amongst strangers: amongst his friends he was free and easy; and his conversation sprightly and entertaining. In domestic life, he was the affectionate husband, the tender parent, the kind master, the hospitable neighbour, and sincere friend; and both by his doctrine and example, a faithful and worthy minister of the parish over which he presided.' To these generalities one might add that he married in 1743 a Dorothea Fancourt, daughter of the Rev. Mr Fancourt of Kilmcote in Leicestershire, and that his affection as a husband and tenderness as a parent sufficed to rear seven children. He received the livings of Harbury and Chesterton, near Leamington, in 1746, and became vicar of Snitterfield in 1754. His wife having died in 1751, he married a second time in 1759, and passed a placid life varied by mild literary composition, dying still as vicar of Snitterfield and being buried in the church there in 1781. Lady Luxborough's experiences were more painful. When Shenstone knew her, she was, as Graves wrote, 'not living on terms of the most perfect conjugal felicity with her Lord'. She was a half-sister of Lord Bolingbroke, being one of the children of Sir Henry St John's second marriage. In 1727 she married Robert Knight, whose father, the cashier of the South Sea Company, had been forced to escape to France and was not permitted to return until 1742.

The two children of her marriage were placed under the care of Lady Hertford, her greatest friend, for she herself was forced against her will by her husband to spend a great part of her time in France. Lady Hertford, later Duchess of Somerset, was to become a patroness of Thomson and Shenstone, a collector of Italian sculpture, connoisseur of art and literature, devotee of Whitefield, and pietist correspondent of the Methodist Lady Huntingdon. Meanwhile, Robert Knight thought fit to suggest that his lady was unfaithful. He was himself, said a contemporary, 'unquestionably a man devoid of morals who roved from fair to fair, and was perhaps glad of an excuse to quit his wife'. Rumour eventually picked out two candidates for the position of co-respondent; one Dr John Dalton, tutor to Lady Hertford's son, who also 'arranged' *Comus* for the stage with the help of Arne's music; and the other, fantastically enough, Shenstone himself, who was only twenty-two and still an obscure farmer's son. As a result, Henrietta Knight was separated from her husband—he became Lord Luxborough in 1746—and exiled to the seat of Barrels-in-Arden, forbidden to travel out of England, to go near London, or to visit the Hertfords. The unfortunate, and almost certainly guiltless, lady spent the rest of her life quietly, dividing her attentions between the embellishment of her estate, the exchange of correspondence, and the occasional composition of pleasant but unremarkable verses, until she died in 1756.

The other member of Shenstone's coterie who needs

a word of mention is Anthony Whistler, who came of an old-established Berkshire family which had possessed the manor of Whitchurch in Oxfordshire on the Thames opposite Pangbourne since 1605. He was born in 1714, and educated at Eton, before proceeding to Oxford in 1732. At that time he was described as 'a young man of great delicacy of sentiment', and twenty years later still preserved this characteristic so far as to live 'in elegant style, and evince a refined taste and softness of manners'. Like Shenstone, he took no degree, but retired to his native Whitchurch, from which he made fairly frequent visits to London, Oxford, or Bristol. His mother had married a second time in 1726, becoming the wife of the Rev. Samuel Walker, rector of Whitchurch from 1723 to 1768, and as these two occupied the manor, they fitted out Whistler himself with a little house of his own, where he lived as a dilettante bachelor. Shenstone visited him at Whitchurch in 1751 and afterwards complained of 'too much punctilio', the result being a temporary estrangement. But by October 1752 their friendship was on its former footing; Whistler, staying at Bristol in the spring of 1754, meditated a visit to The Leasowes in the summer, but was taken ill and died on 10 May.

And finally, the Lytteltons. Shenstone's main contact with this family, who occupied Hagley Hall, just over the brow of the Clent Hills, about four miles west of The Leasowes, came about through George, 'the good Lord Lyttelton', who was the eldest son of Sir Thomas, and who succeeded his father in 1751. He was nearly six years older than Shenstone, and preceded him by the same interval at Oxford. His career included the Grand Tour, a seat in the Commons for Okehampton, vigorous opposition to Walpole, a seat on the Treasury Board, membership of the Privy Council, and the Chancellorship of the Exchequer. Chesterfield joined him in his political opposition to Walpole, but held up his social awkwardness as a warning to his son. His literary work achieved a slight pre-eminence with the *Dialogues of the Dead* and the *Monody* to the memory of his wife; he received the admiring dedication of Fielding's *Tom Jones* in 1749, published the collected works of his friend James Thomson in 1750, and helped to establish *The World*. Through intermarriages the Lyttelton family connected itself with those of the Pitts, Grenvilles, Wests, and Cobhams—names which make frequent appearances in Shenstone's correspondence.

Such were the chief members of Shenstone's circle of friends, occupying a small place in the world's eye, but representing sufficiently well its normal rural and literary culture. It was from such a narrow circle that he started to rise, as Graves said, 'from a state of the utmost obscurity to so great a degree of celebrity and repute'. Meanwhile, he enjoyed a variety of amusements. About 1735 he had visited Richard Graves' elder brother, Morgan, who dwelt with his sister at Mickleton in Gloucestershire, and to whose house there resorted all the lively company of the neighbourhood. Despite his aversion to cards and dancing, Shenstone was susceptible enough, and though he successfully withstood the charms of a romping maiden, who 'could hardly extort a smile from [his] impenetrable reserve', yet, as a punishment for this insensibility, he languished for the mild and serene graces of Miss Graves, who, it appears, inspired her votaries with 'a melancholy languor, which vented itself in sighs and moans, plaintive love-songs and elegies of woe'. What impediment there was is not recorded, but it is certain that marriage would have rendered the poet's £300 a year disastrously inadequate, and forced him to the uncongenial efforts of work, literary or otherwise. The same difficulty no doubt arose on a later occasion, when in 1743 he fell in love with a certain Miss C(arter?) at Cheltenham. So he remained un-married, and managed in the love-songs inscribed to Flavia, Delia, Daphne, Ophelia, Iris, or Roxana, to approach the delicacy of Prior, and discreetly to suppress all traces of those poignant feelings which the gentle passion is said to have inspired.

Visits to London also varied the round of country life. His first visit there was made in January 1741, to negotiate for the publication of his *Judgment of Hercules*, and caused him great excitement. He stayed with a Mr Wintle, a perfumer, near Temple Bar. For the first few months of the year his letters frequently refer to politics and the theatre. He saw Cibber in Congreve's *Old Batchelor*, and the comedian Quin as Falstaff, both at Drury Lane, found *The*

Merry Wives of Windsor disappointing, and read
large numbers of pamphlets occasioned by the famous
anti-Walpole motion of 13 February, when Carteret
and Sandys rose 'to beseech his Majesty to remove
Sir Robert Walpole from his presence and councils
for ever'. He paid other visits during the early part
of 1742, 1743 and 1744, and in the first of these years
was there for a considerable time, at least from March
until August. He liked to escape from The Leasowes
in winter; the summers there afforded him frequent
pleasure, but the winters were dreary and lonely. He
complains in November 1742 that 'I am so unhappy
in my wintery, unvisited state, that I can almost say
with Dido, "tædet cœli convexa tueri". I am
miserable, to think that I have not thought enough
to amuse me. I walk a day together; and have no
idea, but what comes in at my eyes.' He nearly
always views autumn and winter with despondency,
and later, in April 1754, writes to Graves that 'the
severity, the duration, the solitude, of this winter'
have exhausted his spirits; in November 1748 he
apologizes to Lady Luxborough for disliking autumn
—'It is not *Youth*, God knows, but a kind of premature Old-Age that makes me bid Autumn less
welcome than I shou'd otherwise do. I am *afraid*
now of what I have hitherto sought opportunities of
indulging; I mean, that pleasing melancholy which
suits my Temper *too well*....Autumn obtrudes its
pensive Look in every nook & Corner. If it paints my
Grove with ever so many colours, those Colours are
so many symptoms of *Decay*.'

Meanwhile, however, he had taken the first step towards the improvement of his estate. He cut a straight walk through his wood at The Leasowes, terminating in a small stone building, and he had created a 'hermitage' in a marle pit, among some hazels, ornamented with a little wooden cross. One only wishes to be able to appropriate from the story of Columella to that of Shenstone the account of the hermit who turns up for employment, 'a very venerable figure, with a long white beard, a bald head, and dressed in a long brown coat almost down to his ancles', who had lost his occupation as an ornament of Sir Humphrey Whimwham's grounds because he debauched the dairy-maid, and was found by reverent visitors consoling himself more frequently with a pipe and jug than with a book of devotions.

These humble beginnings soon germinated into a more elaborate plan. A certain Philip Southcote at Wooburn had displayed the beauties of his estate by planning a 'belt' to encircle an area of farmland. The belt consisted wholly of land out of cultivation, part of it wooded, part the valleys of rivulets; and through it ran a path diversified with grottoes and other dainty devices, while views across the farmland within the circumference of the path, and over the countryside beyond its bounds, provided the charms of unaffected nature. It was, as Thomas Whately remarked in his *Observations on Modern Gardening*, 'literally a grazing farm lying round the house; and a walk, as unaffected and as unadorned as a common

field path...conducted through the several enclosures.' 'Deck'd by thee', said William Mason's
English Garden more ponderously to Southcote:

> Deck'd by thee,
> The simplest Farm eclips'd the Garden's pride,
> Even as the virgin blush of innocence
> The harlotry of Art.

The idea of the 'belt' was not, perhaps, perfect in
all respects: Uvedale Price later complained that the
wretched visitor who was entrapped into it, and had
to perform the whole circle in the improver's company, would soon 'allow that a snake with its tail in
its mouth is comparatively but a faint emblem of
eternity'. But in the 1730's the invention was an
exciting one. The idea passed from Southcote to
Morgan Graves *via* a Mr Morgan of Essex, a distant
relative; Graves carried out some improvements at
Mickleton, and Mickleton fired Shenstone's imagination. For this mode of design, so harmonious with
the prevailing trend towards the natural, he felicitously invented the term 'landskip garden'.
Henceforth, it was the principal interest of his life
to educate his grounds in order to clarify their
potential beauties, to provide himself with an
agreeable retreat, and to engage the esteem of a
pleasant circle of friends.

His retirement became later the subject of much
comment. For many years every writer who sketched
the history of gardening felt bound to refer to him,

either with praise for a virtuous and well-chosen life, or with blame for an anti-social whim. Graves was able to draw moral lessons about the self-induced misery of the recluse; Gray, Walpole and Johnson, as already mentioned, looked with pity on a man trying to build without straw for his bricks. That this eventually became Shenstone's own view there can be little doubt, though sometimes he was able to congratulate himself on the social success which he achieved: 'I look upon my scheme of embellishing my farm as the only lucky one I ever pursued in my life.—My place now brings the world home to me, when I have too much indolence to go forth in quest of it.' More frequently, however, he lamented his lack of energy and occupation. But to others the compensations of an independent life of self-determined development seemed to outweigh its disadvantages. His friends—Jago, Lady Luxborough, Whistler, Robert Dodsley and Thomas Percy— looked on with admiration; aristocratic acquaintances sought his advice on the improvement of their estates; theorists of gardening like Thomas Whately found in The Leasowes 'a perfect picture of his mind, simple, elegant, and amiable', and Joseph Heely, in his *Letters on the Beauties of...The Leasowes* in 1777, commended 'the hospitable, the generous, the immortal Shenstone! whose private character did so much to honour humanity; whose public one, in the literary world as a poet and a man of consummate knowledge, ranks so estimable; and to whose exquisite taste is wholly owing the inimitable beauties that rise in THE LEASOWES.' And if the final charge were made that a brief retirement from the world is an excellent refreshment, but a prolonged one an escape from responsibility, he might reply, in the words of a more famous gardener: 'cela est bien dit; mais il faut cultiver notre jardin.'

PART II

THE QUEST OF THE SHARAWADGI—
A DIGRESSION

Had I not observed that Purblinde men have discoursed well
of Sight, and some without issue excellently of Generation,
I that was never master of any considerable garden had not
attempted this Subject: But the Earth is the Garden of Nature,
and each fruitful Countrey a Paradise.

SIR THOMAS BROWNE, *The Garden of Cyrus*

The fact that Shenstone's first improvement was the
creation of a straight walk was gently ironical. This
straightness was the only feature in all the estate
which later caused any misgivings. 'Whether to
plant a walk in undulating curves...demands any
great powers of mind, I will not enquire', said
Johnson; but gardeners of the natural school knew
without enquiring that to plant a straight walk
needed no powers of mind at all. When Shenstone
was young, however, the doctrine of the serpentine
line was still nebulous, and it remained so until 1753,
when Hogarth's well-timed *Analysis of Beauty:
written with a view of fixing the fluctuating Ideas of
Taste*, fixed them only too well. The 'serpentine line'
which Hogarth advocated was thereafter so popular
that even later theorists of the picturesque, like
Uvedale Price, were annoyed by its continual re-
iteration. It is worth a little effort, on the threshold

of The Leasowes, to recall the main steps by which irregularity came into its own.

'The Chineses', said Sir William Temple, in his essay *Upon the Gardens of Epicurus* (1685), are moved to sarcasm by European gardens in the symmetrical manner. This surprising revelation reverberated down the eighteenth century. 'The Chineses', Temple continued, 'scorn this way of Planting, and say a Boy that can tell an Hundred, may plant Walks of Trees in strait Lines, and over-against one another, and to what Length and Extent he pleases.' Not only that, but their sensibility was so far advanced, that they had a word for a phenomenon of which the very idea had hardly penetrated to Europe —the phenomenon of beauty occurring in the absence of discernible order or recurrent design. The word was 'Sharawadgi'. If they came upon a garden which struck the imagination with its unmathematical beauty, they would exclaim: 'The Sharawadgi is fine, or is admirable.' Sharawadgi seemed the *ne plus ultra* of aesthetic propriety.

The word did not acclimatize itself in eighteenth-century aesthetics. Though the century's additions to the vocabulary might form an illuminating chapter —'etiquette, persiflage, ennui; picturesque, and sentimental; Dark Ages, Middle Ages, intolerance'— 'Sharawadgi' would not be found among them. It was a little too difficult to digest. But as a symbol of the basic phenomenon in naturalistic aesthetics— design which is not design—it is a useful, even a picturesque, label for a complex of ideas.

The Englishman's grasp of Chinese principles did not, perhaps, appreciate their esoteric subtlety. They depended on an abstruse philosophy, the aesthetic of Feng Shui (wind-water), which, says Professor Patrick Abercrombie in *Town and Country Planning*, produced probably the most elaborately composed landscape which has ever existed, a landscape which had to preserve certain spiritual values and also to fulfil the practical purpose of supporting a dense population. The relations between humanity and the land were formulated in a series of precise rules, the science of 'adapting the residence of the living and the dead so as to co-operate and harmonize with the local currents of the cosmic Breath'. The main point is that the Chinese recognized artificiality, and consciously accepted and admired it, as Chinese painting, though asymmetrical and apparently 'free', is formal in accepting the rules of an elaborate tradition. The naturalism of the English garden was quite a different thing: it is curious that it should have been defended by reference to an aesthetic which the Englishman did not realize, which, had he realized, he could not have understood, and which, had he understood, he could never have practised.

Without pretending to exhaustiveness, it may be said that Sharawadgi, as understood in England, has three main ingredients. In the first place, it has no faith in mathematics and deifies irregularity. In the second, it finds beauty in infinite variety. In the third, it treats natural material according to that material's own potential organic pattern.

[41]

To disentangle these components, and treat each of them separately, would require great skill in analysis. Fortunately, they need not be disentangled here. On the whole, they involve each other and co-exist, though a garden can be unmathematical without being varied, as Uvedale Price complained; it can be varied without being irregular—as when it embodies Hogarth's serpentine line; it can be irregular without treating naturally its natural material. (This last fact aroused satirists to almost endless mirth.) So, having noted that the divisions made above do not merely mark distinctions without differences, we may consider them as included under the general attack on mathematics.

Temple's own preference lay decidedly towards formality. He was an enthusiastic cultivator of fruit, for which neatness and order were necessary. Like Evelyn, whose descriptions of gardens always concern themselves with waterworks, avenues, borders, orangeries, and similar delights, he found that the tastes of his own generation suited him well. He believed the finest shape for a garden to be that of a square or an oblong, and described at length the beauties of Moor Park, in Hertfordshire, where laurels, gravel-walks, and flights of stone steps, gave all the graces of a noble symmetry, and produced, he said, 'the sweetest Place, I think, that I have seen in my Life'. 'The Remembrance of what it was, is too pleasant ever to forget, and therefore I do not believe to have mistaken the Figure of it, which may serve for a Pattern to the best Gardens of our

[42]

Manner, and that are most proper for our Country and Climate.' And though he conceded that irregular gardens might possibly be more beautiful than regular ones, he believed them far more difficult to achieve. There were rules for designing a formal garden, and any one might achieve a high measure of success; but in the irregular mode, with its unknown perils, there were twenty chances of disastrous failure for one of success. It was safer, he concluded, to be geometrical.

But Temple was one of the latest to approve what Sir Thomas Browne called 'this elegant ordination of vegetables'. And he came in for sorrowful reproof from William Mason, who pointed out the faults of his perfect garden:

> Thou shalt not find
> One blade of verdure, but with aching feet
> From terras down to terras shalt descend
> Step following step, down tedious flights of stairs.

The revelation that the Chinese, particular *arbitri elegantiarum* of the eighteenth century, scorned the gardening tastes of Le Roi Soleil and William III was embarrassing. And any one who had never read Temple's essay could find its rankling exposure repeated in the *Spectator* (No. 414). Addison quotes Temple almost literally, though without acknowledgment, when he describes the Chinese who laugh at the plantations of Europe because they hold that 'any one may place trees in equal rows and uniform figures'. If 'any one' could do what Le Nôtre had spent all his energies to perfect, it was time either to admit that Europe was inferior to Asia in matters of taste, or to call on the more original geniuses of William Kent or 'Capability' Brown. The reputation of the 'quincuncial lozenge, or net-work plantations of the ancients', seemed in the face of this Oriental superciliousness to be blasted for ever. The Englishman accepted Temple's information, neglected his cautions, and went after the Sharawadgi; like Nebuchadnezzar in Sir Thomas Browne, 'overdelighted with the bravery of this Paradise, in his melancholy metamorphosis he found the folly of that delight, and a proper punishment in the contrary habitation, in wilde plantings and wandrings of the fields.'

Walpole was later able, in his *Anecdotes of Painting*, to sum up the results of this enlightenment. Canals, balustrades, terraces, vases, appeared in their true light, as the impotent displays of false taste. Art, which in the hands of simple men 'had at first been made a succedaneum to nature', now in the hands of ostentatious wealth had become the means of thwarting her. Even trees suffered mutilation. 'The shears were applied to the lovely wildness of form with which Nature has distinguished each various species of tree and shrub. The venerable oak, the romantic beech, the useful elm, even the aspiring circuit of the lime, the regular round of the chesnut, and the almost moulded orange-tree, were corrected by such fantastic admirers of symmetry.' One saw at once the heinousness of St-Germain, where an actual forest was clipped to conform with the lines of the terrace. 'Waterworks to wet the unwary, not to refresh the panting spectator, and parterres embroidered in patterns like a petticoat' became a witness to one's perverted judgment—almost a reflection on one's morals, for the coincidence of their popularity at the courts of Louis XIV and Charles II could hardly be accidental. Alas, *quantum mutatus*.... On the other hand, natural gardening was a sign of moral integrity just as much as a rustic life itself was: 'quand on pense à ombrager un ravin', said the Prince de Ligne, 'quand on cherche à attraper un ruisseau à la course, on a trop à faire pour devenir citoyen dangereux, général intrigant, et courtisan cabaleur.' As for Shenstone, 'his life was unstained by any crime', Johnson admitted, with an Olympian magnificence of understatement; and if the commendation cannot be applied to all the gentlemen gardeners of the century, their curiosity about their estates at least helped to keep them in paths of quietness and peace. *Bonus agricola, bonus civis.*

The histories of gardening which this renewed interest provoked ran very much after a pattern. They started with the gardens of Alcinous, as described by Homer, and then proceeded to those of Semiramis, who was credited with the building of Babylon and the hanging gardens of Media, to Sennacherib's great park or 'paradise' in Nineveh, and so to the delights of Virgil's *Georgics* and the gardens of Pliny. Then, ignoring the formality of mediaeval gardens and the knots of Elizabethan

[45]

flower-beds, the story leapt to Bacon, Sir Henry Wotton, Milton, Temple, the French and the Dutch. By this analysis it could be proved beyond any doubt that Restoration gardens were degenerate, and the blame could be, and frequently was, laid on the French. Had not England once enjoyed an uncorrupted gardening taste? Had not the royal palaces been surrounded by pleasances uncontaminated by the hand of Art? There was Bacon, whose support was eagerly sought during the eighteenth century for all kinds of causes. His essay *Of Gardens*, while not wholeheartedly anticipating Kent and Brown, was considered on the whole to favour the picturesque school. At least, of 'the Making of *Knots* or *Figures* with *Divers Coloured Earths*' he had scornfully said: 'You may see as good Sights many times in Tarts.' He had disapproved of '*Images Cut out* in *Juniper*, or other *Garden stuffe*'. And he had demanded the third division of his garden to be a heath, 'framed... to a *Naturall wildnesse*'. These points were all mentioned with special approval by William Mason when his poetical survey of horticulture brought him to 'sagest Verulam'.

> 'Twas thine to banish from the royal groves
> Each childish vanity of crisped knot
> And sculptor'd foliage.

There was also Sir Henry Wotton, who earned flattering references on account of two paragraphs in *Reliquiae Wottonianae* (1651), one of which maintained 'a certain contrariety between *building* &

[46]

gardening: For as *Fabricks* should be *regular*, so *Gardens* should be *irregular*, or at least cast into a very wild *Regularity*', and the other contending that the beauty of a garden lay 'rather in a delightfull confusion, then with any plain distinction of the pieces.' That was the very presence of Sharawadgi at home, springing full-armed from the brain of an undegenerate provost of Eton. There was also Milton, blind to the physical world, but seeing the ideal garden with the intellectual eye, so little did he suffer by the loss of sight. 'The vigour of a boundless imagination', said Walpole, when he thought how the poet set Adam and Eve to prune and tend the garden of Eden, 'told him how a plan might be disposed, that would embellish nature, and restore art to its proper office, the just improvement or imitation of it.'

So the attack on geometry had an excellent pedigree. It would be easy to accumulate innumerable references of the same sort. Even Vanbrugh, suspected by the century for his megalomaniac classicism, begged the Duchess of Marlborough in 1707 to retain the ruins of Woodstock Manor as an object of interest in Blenheim Park, and suggested that 'were the inclosure fill'd with trees...promiscuously set to grow up in a wild thicket', so that the ruins could just be perceived among them, 'it wou'd make one of the most Agreable Objects that the best of landskip Painters can invent'. This it is true occurred in a private letter, and was unavailing. But almost at the same time (in 1711) the distinguished advocacy of Shaftesbury's *Characteristicks* was commending 'the rude Rocks, the mossy Caverns, the irregular unwrought *Grotto's*, and broken Falls of Water, with all the horrid graces of the Wilderness itself, as representing Nature more', and as displaying 'a Magnificence beyond the formal Mockery of Princely Gardens'. And then came Addison.

The attack on geometry is perhaps the most significant fact of eighteenth-century aesthetics. The "mystical mathematicks of the City of Heaven" were not enough to save it from disgrace in the garden. This development, following so closely on the most epochal influences which mathematical science has ever exercised, was partly a coincidence, and partly a consequence of the new science itself. It was a coincidence, in that it revolted out of sheer boredom from the geometrical fashions which had reigned since the French apprenticeship of Charles II, and which had been reinforced by the Dutch sympathies of William III. Nature, it seemed, was born free but was everywhere to be found in chains. It was a consequence in that, while mathematical demonstration was removing caprice from the physical universe, it suggested a new reverence for natural forms and processes. It was still possible, of course, to consider nature as wild and unkempt, as needing man's domination; but it was also possible to experience a new respect for her unreformed presence. And a third element in the fresh current of feeling was the replacement of theological awe by deistic admiration. As Geoffrey Scott has written in *The*

Architecture of Humanism, ' a kind of humility, which had once flowed in fixed Hebraic channels, found outlet in self-abasement before the majesty, the wildness, and the infinite complexity, of the physical creation'. One might still, of course, admire as the Stoics had done the *order* of the universe: Samuel Clarke's *Demonstration of the Being and Attributes of God* (1705) glorifies 'the exquisite Regularity of all the Planets' Motions, without Epicycles, Stations, Retrogradations, or any other Deviation or Confusion whatever'. One of the achievements of science was to educe order from arbitrariness. But on the other hand, one could believe that even where there was no visible order, yet there must be an underlying pattern, a reason why things were so and not otherwise. Sir Thomas Browne saw no ugliness in a bear or a toad; Shaftesbury declared that serpents, savage beasts, and poisonous insects, were beautiful in themselves. And by a similar train of reasoning, if a tree chose to grow with a wild luxuriance of form, it became a sacrilege to subject it to a human canon. Pope's famous epistle to Burlington made a point against such perverted taste:

> His Gardens next your admiration call,
> On ev'ry side you look, behold the Wall!
> No pleasing Intricacies intervene,
> No artful Wildness to perplex the scene;
> Grove nods at Grove, each Alley has a brother,
> And half the Platform just reflects the other.
> The suff'ring eye inverted Nature sees,
> Trees cut to Statues, Statues thick as trees.

The new morality counted it a crime to thwart the course of natural growth.

There is plenty of evidence for this; here it is most instructive to consider the *Spectator* papers which Addison wrote on *The Pleasures of the Imagination* (Nos. 411–21). Addison was a most effective populariser of intelligent ideas. Paper 420 admirably expresses the general thrill of reverence which the new science brought to the contemplation of nature. The imagination bowed before the majesty and variety of the universe just as it had previously bowed before the infinite power of God. 'Among this Sett of Writers, there are none who more gratifie and enlarge the Imagination, than the Authors of the new Philosophy', said Addison, at the beginning of a paragraph which recalls his hymn, *The spacious firmament on high.* The reverent awe which so nobly illuminates these passages is the highest reach of his inspiration. It depended largely on the magnitude of the firmament, but it lent an extra assurance to the belief that Nature was superior to Art. The works of art, Addison declared in paper No. 414, 'can have nothing in them of that Vastness and Immensity which afford so great an Entertainment to the Mind of the Beholder'. And he passed on to apply this lesson to the art of gardening. 'There is generally in Nature something more Grand and August, than what we meet with in the Curiosities of Art....On this Account our *English* Gardens are not so entertaining to the Fancy as those in *France* and *Italy*, where we see a large Extent of Ground covered over with an agreeable mixture of Garden and Forest, which represent every where an artificial Rudeness, much more charming than that Neatness and Elegancy which we meet with in those of our own Country.'

In addition to this, he was aware of the more fundamental change in mentality which, on the basis of the discoveries of science, would allow natural phenomena the form that their organic development dictates. 'Our *British* Gardeners...instead of humouring Nature, love to deviate from it as much as possible. Our Trees rise in Cones, Globes, and Pyramids. We see the Marks of the Scissors upon every Plant and Bush. I do not know whether I am singular in my Opinion, but for my own part, I would rather look upon a Tree in all its Luxuriancy and Diffusion of Boughs and Branches, than when it is thus cut and trimmed into a Mathematical Figure; and cannot but fancy that an Orchard in Flower looks infinitely more delightful, than all the little Labyrinths of the most finished Parterre.' Thus Addison clinched his distinguished advocacy of the unmathematical, which, considering *The Spectator's* popularity, was probably the most powerful single influence before the generation of Strawberry Hill.

Walpole's *Anecdotes of Painting* give special credit to No. 173 of *The Guardian*, which appeared the following year, 1713, and was written by Pope. The Guardian himself, in some trepidation, takes a friend to visit his country house. Its simple attractions, however, surpass the elaborations of grander mansions, and the proprietor is able to congratulate himself. 'There is certainly something in the amiable Simplicity of unadorned Nature, that spreads over the Mind a more noble sort of Tranquillity and a loftier Sensation of Pleasure, than can be raised from the nicer Scenes of Art.' After a brief digression to that *locus classicus* the garden of Alcinous, he repeats Addison's complaint against 'the various Tonsure of Greens into the most regular and formal Shapes', and laments that we 'are yet better pleas'd to have our Trees in the most awkward Figures of Men and Animals, than in the most regular of their own'. (Pope, of course, sometimes had tastes more specifically 'romantic'; *Eloisa and Abelard*, as has often been noticed, fostered the vogue for the gloomily and spectacularly macabre.) Not long afterwards, Batty Langley made his bow to the world.

With Batty Langley's advent, naturalism begins to look both triumphant and amusing. His famous *New Principles of Gardening: Or, the Laying out and Planting Parterres, Groves, Wildernesses, Labyrinths, Avenues, Parks, &c., After a more* GRAND *and* RURAL MANNER *than has been done before* appeared in 1728, was dedicated to the King, and was forthrightly directed against 'coxcombs' who were always deviating from Nature instead of imitating it. In 1749, Shenstone writes to Lady Luxborough that he is lending her a book—which he himself borrowed five years before!—by a Mr Langley, which he praises as being written 'when the present *natural* Taste began to dawn', and he comments that 'the Man is something illiterate, but his Notions are not amiss in *many* Respects, I think'. As Langley is one of the few horticulturists whom Shenstone mentions, he may receive a little more attention than his comparative unimportance of itself would justify. As with Bubb Doddington, his name has immortalized him, when his works alone would have been forgotten. Horticulture meant for him the science of '*Walks, Slopes, Borders, Open Plains, Plain Parterres, Avenues, Groves, Wildernesses, Labyrinths, Fruit-Gardens, Flower-Gardens, Vineyards, Hop-Gardens, Nurseries, Coppiced Quarters, Green Openings*, like Meadows: Small Inclosures of *Corn, Cones of Ever-Greens*, of *Flowering Shrubs*, of *Fruit-Trees*, of *Forest-Trees*, and mix'd together: *Mounts, Terraces*, Winding *Valleys, Dales, Purling Streams, Basons, Canals, Fountains, Cascades, Grotto's, Rocks, Ruins, Serpentine Meanders, Rude Coppies* (sic), *Haystacks, Wood-Piles, Rabbit* and *Hare-Warrens, Cold Baths, Aviaries, Cabinets, Statues, Obelisks, Manazeries, Pheasant* and *Partridge-Grounds, Orangeries, Melon-Grounds, Kitchen-Gardens, Physick* or *Herb-Gardens, Orchard, Bowling-Green, Dials, Precipices, Amphi-theatres*, &c.' Is the '&c.', one wonders, a sign of ostentation, or merely of compassion for the reader?

What the imitation of Nature meant for Batty Langley he explains in the Preface. It meant primarily variety; it meant respect for natural configuration; it meant irregularity. He could think of nothing 'more *shocking* than a *stiff, regular Garden*'. The violation of Nature for the sake of geometry was an anguish to him: 'the very great Exactness that

was observed in the laying out these regular Gardens ',
he remarked, introducing a lament whose capitals
and italics would not have disgraced Queen Victoria,
'were (*sic*) often the *Loss* of many *fine Views*, as well
as *sturdy* OAKS, whose *Herculean Aspects*, one would
have thought, should have forbid those *base* and
ignorant Practices. What a Shame it is, to destroy a
noble OAK of two or three Hundred Years Growth,
that always produces a *pleasant Shade*, and graceful
Aspect, for the sake of making *a trifling Grass-Plot*
or *Flower-Knot regular*.' By one of the pleasant
ironies which beset the naturalistic movement,
William Mason, after the picturesque had come into
its own, had to devote a good section of *The English
Garden* to discussing whether one should destroy
ancient oaks, the planters of which had been so
thoughtless as to dispose them in straight rows.
Mason sorrowfully decides that, unless the gardener
can disguise their straightness by judiciously adding
other trees in irregular formation, there is no remedy
but to demolish them root and branch, making
wildernesses of handsome groves, sacrificed upon the
altar of Irregularity. The wheel had come full circle.

Part VI of the *New Principles* launches into general
instructions. Gardens should present new aspects at
every turn to entertain the eye. Walks which do not
open to extensive views should terminate in 'Woods,
Forests, misshapen Rocks, strange Precipices, Mountains, old Ruins, grand Buildings, etc.' The reader
cannot help being charmed and awed by the ease
with which Langley, and the picturesque school in

general, desiderate their Precipices, Mountains, and Ruins. He is Napoleonic in a small way. The situation in addition should be 'bless'd with small Rivulets and purling Streams'. Groves should preserve 'a regular irregularity'—Langley's nearest approach to an aphorism. 'Little walks by purling Streams, in Meadows, and through Corn-Fields, Thickets, etc., are delightful Entertainment.' This method of design he believed '*entirely New*, as well as the most *grand* and *rural*'.

But despite the incense burnt to Nature, man still claims his right to improve. Into the art of garden design, as the formidable prospectus printed above will show, the hand of man is to enter with all its cunning. Canals and fountains are to be admitted, walks at their intersections are to be adorned by 'Statues, large open Plains, Groves, Basons, Fountains, Sun-Dials, and [or?] Obelisks'. He even permits the elevation of artificial mounds, of 'Hills and Dales of easy Ascents', where Nature has been remiss. And he hints pleasantly at local solecisms in deprecating the erection of statues of Neptune on the tops of hills, or of Pan the god of sheep among the fishes of a fountain. For the country mason, one deity was as good as another. One thinks of the Irish poem about the

> heathen goddesses,
> Caesar, Plato, and Nebuchadnezzar,
> All standing naked in the open air.

In the course of this advice, 'open lawns and large

Centers' are found to be designed for 'Minerva and Pallas, goddesses of wisdom', who must have been pleased to encounter one another. The final direction instructs 'Niches to be reserved for *Dii minores*'.

Although Batty Langley is interesting mainly as an amusing curiosity, he unconsciously illustrates the century's dilemma. He maintains in one breath that the imitation of Nature means as close a dependence as possible on the materials and organic development of unimproved landscape, and, in the next, that architectural adornments and artificial mounds are permissible. Is this just an instance of the confusion which naturally overtakes such eclectic thought as formed the background of English ideas throughout the century, or has it an order of its own?

The fact that there are, of course, several contributory influences suggests that the whole matter is a confusion—the confusion of a transition. *On prend son bien où on le trouve*. But a few general principles may be formulated. There is a half-way house in the progress towards the natural—it is the belief that anything is admissible except geometry. As a result, while straight walks are unpardonable, it becomes perfectly proper to erect what one enthusiast, the self-styled 'Mons. D'Alenzon', writing *The Bonze, or Chinese Anchorite, an Oriental Epic Novel* in 1769, called 'a palace in the free taste of China, which, tied to no partial rules, admitted all the beauties of architecture'. While clipped trees are an impiety committed in the innermost shrine of Nature, an artificial cascade, as long as it successfully

[56]

deceives the eye, is a matter for pride and congratulation.

> Doubtless the pleasure is as great
> In being cheated, as to cheat.

An avenue is unpardonable; a hermitage attracts the most reverent attention, for, remarks William Gilpin in his *Observations relative chiefly to Picturesque Beauty*, 'it is not every one that can build a ruin'. Anything might occur except recurrence, and the saving graces of Sharawadgi covered a multitude of sins.

This compromise with Nature was not quite as illogical as it sounds. It would require a great deal of space to deal adequately with aesthetic vagaries in this matter. But to understand how human agency was permitted to interpose in the realization of natural designs is to understand one of the meanings which the century attached to that elusive term 'Nature'.

For if Nature had her own laws on which man was not to impose an unsympathetic pattern, at least the reverence which the age showed for her did not exceed that of Aristotle; and for Aristotle Nature was a force of potential achievement rather than an actual fulfilled perfection. Nature is the principle of growth —in each object the source of its own production and development. A natural object develops towards a goal—no other objects do this. 'In general Art partly completes what Nature is unable to elaborate, and partly imitates her.' The section of the *Physics* which contains this definition (192^b 8) is followed up by a discussion of the limiting forces which control this natural impulse. Just as health is an end of Nature which is often thwarted by the inherent flaws in the material in which Nature has to manifest itself, so with all things that are subject to growth. The higher in the scale, the more necessary is human agency to assist Nature, until in the case of the human being a long period of care and training is essential. Art imitates Nature, then, in that it carries on and reinforces the impulse towards perfection; it imitates, or approximates itself to, the creative force and productive principle of the universe. The function of the imagination is to see the universal perfections towards which Nature, hampered by the perversion of accidents, is tending.

The prestige of artistic creation, therefore, was due, in the eyes of the eighteenth century, to the fact that it could present scenes in perfect balance and mass, that it was selective of the rude materials of unassisted Nature, as much as to any technical virtuosity. 'I believe one is generally sollicitous for a kind of ballance in a landskip', wrote Shenstone, 'and, if I am not mistaken, the painters generally furnish one: A building, for instance, on one side, contrasted by a group of trees, a large oak, or a rising hill on the other.' Irregularity was reverenced merely to the point of substituting an implicit for an explicit symmetry. And consequently the more a natural scene approximated to the composition of a picture the more 'natural' it was. Aware of this, Addison wrote that 'tho' there are several of these wild Scenes, that are more delightful than any artificial Shows; yet we find the Works of Nature still more pleasant, the more they resemble those of Art: Hence it is that we take Delight...in any thing that hath such a Variety or Regularity as may seem the Effect of Design in what we call the Works of Chance.' And, therefore, it follows, that if man, by using the materials of Nature with greater agility and flexibility than she herself can command, can, while concealing the hand of artifice, realize that design which is implied in potential natural beauty, it is his duty and privilege to do so. And this leads Addison to a remarkable anticipation of Shenstone's speciality, the *ferme ornée*. 'Why may not a whole Estate be thrown into a kind of Garden by frequent Plantations, that may turn as much to the Profit, as the Pleasure of the Owner? A Marsh overgrown with Willows, or a Mountain shaded with Oaks, are not only more beautiful, but more beneficial, than when they lie bare and unadorned. Fields of Corn make a pleasant Prospect, and if the Walks were a little taken care of that lie between them, if the natural Embroidery of the Meadows were helpt and improved by some small Additions of Art, and the several Rows of Hedges set off by Trees and Flowers, that the Soil was capable of receiving, a Man might make a pretty Landskip of his own Possessions.' No closer description could be given of the means and methods of Shenstone's achievements.

So the eighteenth century started off on its most difficult artistic task, the Quest of the Sharawadgi. William Kent (1684–1748) was well qualified to lead the pilgrimage. 'Painter enough to taste the charms of landscape, bold and opinionative enough to dare and to dictate', he started from the standpoint of pictorial art and, in Walpole's famous phrase, 'leapt the fence and saw that all nature was a garden'. The fence, it is true, had become less formidable; Vanbrugh and Bridgeman had employed the ha-ha, so that the countryside could be considered as an extension of the garden. Kent appeared on the scene at a fortunate moment; so unsuccessful as a painter that even his friends could raise no enthusiasm, he had sufficient social aplomb to win the Earl of Burlington's eye, and, probably through him, to meet Pope. How far he was inspired by the poet's famous garden and grotto at Twickenham is not clear: Walpole thinks that they 'undoubtedly contributed' to influence him, through the variety of moods which they were designed to arouse. At any rate the principles expressed in Pope's *Epistle to Burlington* were close to Kent's heart. By variety, contrast, and surprise he approximated landscape to the forms of painting, the most notorious reach of his exuberance being the planting of dead trees in Kensington Gardens to imitate the landscapes of Salvator Rosa. Nature, unlike the child at the emancipated school who cried because she was forced to do what she liked, could not protest against this unnatural naturalness. As a result, wrote Walpole, 'adieu to canals, circular basons, and cascades tumbling down marble steps, that last absurd magnificence of Italian and French villas.... The gentle stream was taught to serpentise seemingly at its pleasure....Dealing in none but the colours of nature, and catching its most favourable features, men saw a new creation opening before their eyes. The living landscape was chastened or polished, not transformed.' Kent specialized in the natural flow of water, in gentle undulations of line, in the preservation of the landscape's rhythmical flow, adorned and punctuated by clumps of trees, sometimes indeed too uniform and too small, but generally planned to obliterate what was unsightly, to vary what was monotonous, or to emphasize what was interesting. When one thinks how Claude employed trees in a foreground to frame his landscape, it is easy to see why Walpole associated him with Kent.

Two of Kent's spiritual heirs kept his ideals flourishing until the Romantic Revival was in full swing. 'Capability' Brown (1715–83) improved on his master's aims, and developed the undulations of natural landscape with greater originality, while his successor Humphrey Repton (1752–1818) perfected the art and left a concise summary of its aims: 'to improve the scenery of a country and to display its native beauties with advantage.' As a result, to the Continent the *Jardin anglais*, which had in the days of Le Nôtre meant the height of formality, came to mean precisely the opposite. 'Nous appelons les jardins de l'ordre pittoresque *jardins anglais*, parce que les Anglais sont les premiers qui en adoptèrent le goût', wrote a M. Curten, in an *Essai sur les Jardins* in 1807. In the course of the change there came the stage of which The Leasowes is representative, when, having disposed of the sumptuousness of Versailles, and not having reached the freedom of the Romantic Revival, the garden could assume a character truly consistent with the well-bred Virgilian rusticity which its gentlemen cultivators so elegantly embodied in themselves. Nature was to obey an etiquette, to move with a decorous and well-bred grace. The change was not from geometry to anarchy, but from rigidity to a graceful suppleness. Or, to look at it in another way, man renounced a despotism over Nature in favour of a mandate to assist her self-development. Shaftesbury, despite his passion for things of a natural kind, understood this when he admired the finer Italian gardens, with their harmonies 'that silently express such order, peace, and sweetness'. It was the chastened elegance of silent good form.

The exact definition of this decorum, it is true, remained obscure. But the eighteenth-century gentleman had made the pilgrimage of the Grand Tour to the shrine of Connoisseurship, and he naturally believed that in its visual aspects the country-side should obey the canons of painting. Uvedale Price's book, to give it its full title, was *An Essay on the Picturesque as compared with the Sublime and the Beautiful; and on the use of studying pictures for the purpose of improving real landscape.* There it was that man had most completely carried out the Aristotelean formula, had eliminated the accidents which thwart Nature's development, and imposed instead a discreet formality, a harmony of atmosphere and rhythm.

The development of the formal appreciation of landscape is a very complex subject, with a great deal of cross-fertilization between Italy, France, Holland and Britain, and between painting, poetry, landscape gardening, the Grand Tour and a classical education. All these influences interact in complicated ways; priority is difficult to establish, and would hardly be illuminating if we knew it. The growth of appreciation was affected by the appeal of painting, which in turn affected poetry—Thomson's *Seasons* are essentially pictorial in their methods—which in turn, and along with painting, affected the way in which people *looked at* scenery. In *The Picturesque; Studies in a Point of View*, Christopher Hussey suggests that the genesis of the picturesque lies at that point in consciousness when the visual qualities of landscape first appeal to the imagination instead of the reason —that is, when the eyes are used to arouse feeling rather than to gain information. As self-preservation antedates aesthetic pleasure—as a general rule, though not perhaps in some individual cases—this luxury demands a measure of social security. This stage is clearly attained at very different periods even within the same country. Appreciation for the Lake District, despite the admiration of sensitive observers like Gray, was late in developing, as compared with the earlier liking for the South (Milton's *L'Allegro*; Denham's *Cooper's Hill*; and so on). Even as late as 1800, John Housman's *Descriptive Tour*, *and Guide to the Lakes*, could describe Borrowdale as 'replete with hideous grandeur', and looking 'as if in this corner of the universe, old Nature had deposited her rubbish during the formation of some happier district'.

Whatever the precise stages were, it is obvious that the English eighteenth century was deeply conditioned in its responses to Nature by the realism of Dutch painting—especially that of Hobbema and Ruysdael—by the engravings of Rembrandt, and by the ideal landscapes of Claude, Gaspar Poussin, and Salvator Rosa, the century's holy trinity. The fact that the English picturesque was almost entirely derivative was sometimes strangely ignored by patriots, and by foreigners suffering from Anglomania. 'Le pittoresque', says Stendhal, in the *Mémoires d'un Touriste*, 'comme les bonnes diligences et les bateaux à vapeur, nous vient d'Angleterre.... Un beau paysage fait partie de la religion comme de l'aristocratie d'un Anglais.' If it were so, England was merely repaying a debt contracted a long while before. The craze spread from England, but, as Addison shows, Englishmen were conscious that France and Italy were in many respects more 'picturesque' than their own country. And 'il riposo di Claudio' and the 'terrible sublime' of Salvator comprised for fifty years the alpha and omega of British Nature-worship. It is almost true to say that the country-side existed in order to be painted—or at least described according to the canons of painting. And the Grand Tour also played its part. An age learns less quickly than its artists, and the Englishman, prior to his Grand Tour, may have felt towards the landscapes of Poussin and Claude and Salvator a conventional reverence with a slight tinge of scepticism: then, while crossing the Alps, or arriving in Italy, he would experience the joy and social relief of a full conviction. Something of the sort can be sensed when Addison compares the works of Nature with those of Art. There is a double pleasure involved if we find a natural scene which resembles a picture: 'We are pleased as well with comparing their Beauties, as with surveying them, and can represent them to our Minds, either as Copies or Originals' (*Spectator*, No. 414). As Aristotle said, 'Ah, that is he!'

The belief that the country-side was designed in order to be painted persisted with virility, from the time when Vanbrugh, called in to design the park at Blenheim, declared that a landscape painter would be the proper executant. The criterion employed in William Gilpin's *Observations relative...to Picturesque Beauty* (written in 1772) is whether the subject can be 'formed into any of those pleasing combinations which constitute a picture'. Horace Walpole, seeing Kent's garden at Stanstead, could hardly believe that Claude had not painted his scenes from it. And in 1798 Jane Austen describes how the Tilneys conduct Catherine Morland round Beechen Cliff, 'viewing the country with the eyes of persons accustomed to drawing, and deciding on its capability of being formed into pictures, with all the eagerness of real taste'.

Finally, the picturesque movement was strengthened by the century's most fashionable psychological discovery—that of the association of ideas, whereby the penumbra of responses involved in artistic appreciation was given due recognition. The notion in its simple form was probably ancient; at any rate, as far as the eighteenth century went, Addison had maintained that the ancients felt a pleasure deeper than ours in reading the poets—'they lived as it were on fairy Ground, and conversed in an enchanted Region, where every Thing they look'd on appear'd Romantic, and gave a thousand pleasing Hints to their Imagination' (*Discourse on Ancient and Modern Learning*). But the idea gained extra prestige when it was linked with associational psychology. David Hartley's *Observations on Man* (1749), one of the most important psychological works of the century, devoted a section to the *Pleasures and Pains of the Imagination*. Among the former was found the beauty of natural scenery, which, Hartley explained, depended on the enrichment of the visual impression by associated pleasurable sensations derived from the other senses, from cheerful memories of country occupations, from comparisons between the disease and squalor of cities and the 'Health, Tranquillity, and Innocence' of country life, from religious awe, and from the agreeable titillation of contemplating mountains and precipices from a situation of perfect safety. Besides this, we transfer on to the works of nature 'part of the Lustre borrowed from Works of Art', and intensify our response to natural beauty by associated aesthetic pleasures. 'Poetry and Painting are much employed in setting forth the Beauties of the natural World, at the same time that they afford us a high degree of Pleasure from many other Sources. Hence the Beauties of Nature delight Poets and Painters and such as are addicted to the Study of their Works, more than others.' The *Observations* had an even wider circulation when abridged by Priestley (1775). The full and final enunciation of the principle as applied to Art came through Richard Payne Knight's *Principles of Taste* (1805), which explained how the response to poetry, painting, or landscape was heightened by the memory of associated beauties. Acquaintance with Theocritus or Virgil will give an added relish to a pastoral landscape. Acquaintance with painting is a prerequisite for a taste in the picturesque. 'This very relation to painting expressed by the word *Picturesque* is that which affords the whole pleasure derived from association.' The emotional overcharge depends on a continual comparison by the eye between Nature and Art, combining the satisfaction derived from the original with that from the skill with which the original is reproduced.

In return, of course, it was expected that such reverent treatment of Nature would inspire a school of landscape artists. William Kent had already bridged the narrow gap between painting and the gardening art, and it was natural to hope that the benefits would be reciprocal. And so while Richard

Wilson, living in a wretched lodging in Tottenham Street, too poor to buy paint or brushes for his rare commissions, was asking James Barry if he knew any one mad enough to employ a landscape painter, Walpole looked briskly forward to a great school of artists. 'In the mean time, how rich, how gay, how picturesque, the face of the country! The demolition of walls laying open each improvement, every journey is made through a succession of pictures; and even where taste is wanting in the spot improved, the general view is embellished by variety.... Enough has been done to establish such a school of landscape, as cannot be found on the rest of the globe. If we have the seeds of a Claud or a Gaspar among us, he must come forth. If wood, water, groves, vallies, glades, can inspire poet or painter, this is the country, this is the age, to produce them. The flocks, the herds, that are now admitted into, now graze on the borders of our cultivated plains, are ready before the painter's eyes, and groupe themselves to animate his picture.' The Quest of the Sharawadgi had ended in this, a rich and exciting sense of liberation and expectancy. The next fifteen years saw the births of Crome (1768), Girtin (1773), Turner (1775), and Constable (1776).

PART III

THE CASTLE OF INDOLENCE

Truly, shepherd, in respect of itself it is a good life; but in respect that it is a shepherd's life, it is nought. In respect that it is solitary, I like it very well; but in respect that it is private, it is a very vile life. Now, in respect it is in the fields, it pleaseth me well; but in respect it is not in the court, it is tedious. As it is a spare life, it fits my humour well; but as there is no plenty in it, it goes much against my stomach.

TOUCHSTONE.

Like most of his educated contemporaries, Shenstone was interested in aesthetic theory. He wrote to Graves, on 19 April 1754, that the reading of Hogarth's *Analysis of Beauty* had 'in some measure adjusted my notions with regard to beauty in general'. The Harvard University Library possesses his copy of Burke's *Philosophical Enquiry into the Origin of our Ideas of the Sublime and Beautiful* (1757), and on Section xv of Part 3, which is entitled *Gradual Variation*, Shenstone has commented, 'coincides wth Hogs Doctrine of the serpentine Line ∿'. This, however, merely corroborates what is clear enough from other indications. He also mentions Hutcheson (whose famous *Inquiry into the Original of our Ideas of Beauty and Virtue* appeared in 1725) and Gerard (author of an *Essay on Taste* [1759] which gave

[69]

prominence to the principle of association). But he began to take a practical interest in The Leasowes long before the influence of Hogarth and Burke affected the course of taste. According to Graves, his fame as a gardener antedated his reputation as a poet, though the Oxford volume of 1737 had been followed in 1741 by *The Judgment of Hercules* and in 1742 by the revised version of *The Schoolmistress*. The influx of visitors, introduced partly through those sympathetic but slightly over-eminent neighbours the Lytteltons, who sometimes overshadowed him, and partly through the respect of many who appreciated natural beauty, seems to 'have made him as much known and admired for his writings in the elegiac and pastoral style, as he was at first for the elegance of his taste in rural embellishments'. The Lytteltons themselves were beautifying Hagley; George Lyttelton had paid Shenstone a visit about 1736, accompanied by Thomas Pitt, the elder brother of the future Lord Chatham—probably out of mere friendly interest, for Shenstone had just come down from Oxford and had as yet done nothing to make himself known. The tentative acquaintanceship lapsed for a while; the poet was not bold enough to accept a general invitation to dine with the Lytteltons whenever he wished; but later, guests from Hagley, the Grenvilles and Pitts and others, would make the short journey to inspect The Leasowes. Shenstone occasionally felt envious at the greater scope for embellishment which his neighbours enjoyed, but the visits of their guests proved a great compensation. 'We, who cannot erect

[70]

fresh temples, or even add a new garden-seat every spring', he writes to Sherrington Davenport on 4 January 1763, 'are obliged to make the most we can of a new and tolerable copy of verses, that costs us *thought* instead of *money*; and even at a pinch to piece out a dull scene with duller poetry: how else could I keep my place in countenance, so near the pompous piles of Hagley? And yet there are few *fashionable* visitants that do not shew an *affection* for the little Amoret, as much as they admire the stately Sacharissa.'

He was impelled towards his schemes of improvement by the example of Morgan Graves at Mickleton, and no doubt partly too from the sheer need to provide himself with an occupation while he was in the country. His earliest surviving letter, dated 19 October 1736, is significant: 'I am, at present, in a very refined State of Indolence and Inactivity. Indeed I make little more Use of a Country Life, than to live over again the Pleasures of *Oxford* and your Company.' He complains in June 1742 of 'the many irksome hours, the stupid identity', which plague him, and in November of the same year protests against his 'wintery, unvisited state'. During the following spring and summer his health remained poor, but he travelled about the country-side and dispelled his gloom. 'When I ride in my chair round my neighbourhood, I am as much stared and wondered at, as a giant would be that should walk through Pall-mall. My vehicle is *at least* as uncommon hereabouts as a blazing comet. My chief pleasure lies in finding out a thousand roads, and delightful little haunts near home, which I never dreamt of: egregious solitudes, and most incomparable bye-lanes! where I can as effectually lose myself within a mile of home, as if I were benighted in the desarts of Arabia.' Occasionally, he took his pleasures less peripatetically; he expressed his approval of the harvesting season to Graves and added: 'I could give my reasons: but you will imagine them to be the activity of country people in a pleasing employment; the full verdure of the summer; the prime of pinks, woodbines, jasmines, &c. I am old, very old' (he was still under thirty) 'for few things give me so much mechanical pleasure as lolling on a bank in the very heat of the sun,

> When the old come forth to play
> On a sun-shine holiday.'

And so, alternating between a listless dissatisfaction and a lively sense of enjoyment, he attempted to banish the one and foster the other by cultivating the art of landscape.

By 1747 or 1748 the improvements had gone some way. George Lyttelton introduced James Thomson to The Leasowes during the summer of 1746; he was 'very facetious, and very complaisant; invited me to his house at Richmond', and both the visitors 'praised my place extravagantly'. During the same summer there were several other visitors, and during the winter the flow continued; Lady Luxborough was expected to reflect her social glory on 'my little walks'. The next year, the developments grew more extensive; following in Southcote's footsteps, Shenstone started to link his beauty-spots together. He mentions his 'terras on the high hill', and improves the appearance of the romantic dell which he christened Virgil's Grove. 'That right friendly bard, Mr Thomson' pays another visit, and promises to bring George Lyttelton with him, so Shenstone cheerfully writes on 21 September to Graves that he lives 'in daily expectations of them and all the world this week'. Lady Luxborough had just been, and left him rejoicing at the sight of a coach with a coronet at his door. His letters are enlivened with a gleeful jubilation whenever any appreciation is shown of his grounds, and if at times there is a trace of petulance when recognition is tardy, it is only fair to recall that they were his *chef d'œuvre*, and that, as gardening taste was only half-educated towards the natural, the visitor might accept as quite fortuitous an effect which was the result of careful thought. When art became too natural, Nature received the praise; and the uninitiated might say, as Partridge remarked of Garrick's acting: 'Why, Lord help me, any man, that is a good man, would have done exactly the same.'

The amusement of rearing livestock was added to the more formal excitements of horticulture. In the spring of 1748, he writes that 'I find no small delight in rearing all sorts of poultry; geese, turkeys, pullets, ducks, &c.' And later, on 15 July 1750, he thanks Lady Luxborough for the present of a couple of geese, one of which objected so strongly to transplantation that she 'fill'd all my Vallies with Complaint for three long Summer's Days'. By the following summer, the improvements at The Leasowes had gained him a considerable reputation; the place began to be, if anything, too renowned, for 'the mob' took a fancy to the flowers which he had planted by his serpentine stream. 'Tho' there are Prim-roses to be gather'd in the Fields in Plenty yet if they can discover one that is apparently planted, they are sure to crop it.' Sunday evenings were a favourite time for pilgrimage; on 9 July 1749 he writes that he has been exhibiting himself as the proud proprietor to a hundred and fifty people, 'and that with no less state and vanity than a Turk in his seraglio'. Fortunately, the 'mob' proved either more literate, more considerate, or more superstitious, than its modern counterpart; and when he inscribed a set of verses purporting to come from the fairies, and to threaten wrongdoers with supernatural punishments, the flower-picking largely ceased.

Meanwhile, he had found a name for the genre he was developing. He called it a *ferme ornée*. This name, he explained to Graves in August 1748, he adopted on the model of the French *parque ornée* (or presumably, a *parc orné*, a *Parque* being a goddess of destiny). The *ferme ornée* wove together, in a negligently subtle way, the illusion of untrammelled pastoral and the pleasing melancholy of human association. The spiritual affinity between this pastoral elegance and the dignities of connoisseurship was of itself almost enough to ensure the fame of The

[74]

Leasowes. It mattered little which painter sprang to mind, as long as the association was made. Graves found the place 'fit for the pencil of a Salvator Rosa'; Mrs Delany linked Shenstone with Claude; George Mason, in his *Essay on Design in Gardening* (1768), thought of Gaspar Poussin. One could hardly avoid the favourite association between painting, poetry, and gardening; The Leasowes were picturesque in the original sense.

A lack of funds, of which he again and again complained, kept Shenstone from drastic alterations. But all that more economical methods could do, he attempted. Flowers appeared in profusion. 'I have been embroidering my Grove with Flowers, till I begin to fear it looks too like a *garden*', he wrote to Lady Luxborough in May 1749. 'If there arrive a Flowering-shrub, it is a Day of rejoicing with me; or (to use a term in *methodism* now so much in Fashion) a *Day of fat Things*.' The next month he wrote to her again; he had planted peonies in his grove, in a 'gloomy Place by the water's side', among ferns and brambles, and found the result delightful. And though major operations, such as went on before his envious eyes at Hagley, were beyond his means, yet he could set his servants to extend his path, 'so that it will now in a short time lead round my whole Farm, &....furnish out a variety of scene in Proportion to its Length' (October 1749, to Lady Luxborough). He could plant trees—which he did to the extent of twenty shillings worth, in March 1750—hazel, hawthorn, crabtree, elder, and some flowering shrubs which were given to him. And he could, to a slight degree, toy with the contemporary fashion for 'Gothic'. A 'Piece of Gothic Architecture' was designed, in June 1749, to cast into the shade all the magnificent schemes of full-blooded Gothicizers like Sanderson Miller, the amateur architect who was a friend of the Lytteltons and of Jago. It was, in fact, a seat above the hermitage, which, in reply to the expenditure of £200 on a rotunda at Hagley, was to cost not less than 'the Sum of fifteen Shillings & Six-pence three farthings'. This formidable threat was followed the same year by the hewing of 'two small Gothick Turrets for my building', which proved so much more troublesome than he expected that they provoked the anathema, 'The Devil take all Gothicism!'—a request to which that gentleman unfortunately turned a deaf ear. This objurgation was turned to serious, though disinterested, concern, in April 1750, when he learnt that Miller was proposing to rebuild Hagley according to a quite incongruous Gothic plan; his sympathies, he explained, ran far more strongly towards the Greek than the Gothic, but his sensibility was forced to suffer in silence. Fortunately, Lady Lyttelton put her foot down and insisted on a house in the Italian style, and Miller had to content himself with erecting a ruined castle in the park, which was commended by Walpole as showing 'the true rust of the Baron's wars'. Shenstone's own flirtation with the new mode took place in remote corners—'a new Gothic-building, or rather a skreen, which cost me ten pounds; and the

[76]

ruins of a Priory, which, however, make a tenant's house, that pays me tolerable poundage.' Had not Horace advised the union of the pleasant with the useful? As for revering the Gothic, Shenstone's affection for it went so far as to collect the material for his own 'ruined' Priory from the remains of Halesowen Abbey. But it was left to Strawberry Hill to try out the new style: The Leasowes remembered their generation, and did not look far into the future.

Occasionally, Shenstone was involved in a brush with the parson. The Rev. Pynson Wilmot was not remarkable for Christian charity, and as he reigned over his parish from 1732 to 1784 he had no doubt plenty of time to discover the failings of his flock. His feelings towards his parishioners were like those of Slender towards Anne Page, that if there were no great love in the beginning, yet heaven might decrease it on better acquaintance, and that upon familiarity would grow more contempt. On one occasion Wilmot managed to stop Shenstone's right of way through a neighbouring coppice, to the detriment of the whole estate. Besides this, Shenstone sometimes had trouble with the tenants, who, having a lenient landlord whom they perhaps considered eccentric, were rather loth to pay their rents. During 1748 the difficulties were stubborn, and, his affairs becoming 'miserably embroiled', he feared that he would have to incommode his indolence and compassion, and arrest one man for three and a half years' arrears. But somehow, with considerable effort, he succeeded in paying his way, and it is probable that the duns who, according to Johnson, haunted his groves, were rather a phantasma or a hideous dream than a reality. Though he was never free from financial anxiety, yet Graves's *Recollection* sufficiently vindicates his employment of his money and repels the suggestion that he was in any serious debt.

Johnson also accused him of neglecting his house. He was certainly more interested in the development of the grounds, and they were what visitors came to see. But he was not negligent indoors; according to Graves he 'acquired two tolerably elegant rooms from a mere farmhouse of a most diminutive dimension'. In the winter of 1748–9, and again in the summer of 1750, he was engaged on operations which he describes to Lady Luxborough: 'the most that I shall gain, will be a Room 17 Feet long, 12 & ½ Broad, and ten Feet two Inches high, the walls plain stucco with a Cornish; a Leaden Pipe conveying water into a Bason at one End over a Slobb: At the other End a Door leading into a Room that (whenever I can afford to finish it) will be my Favourite. As you enter into this last, the Point of Clent-Hill appears visto-Fashion thro' the Door & one of the windows. (The same will be reflected in a Peer-glass at the End of the former Room.) This last Room I purpose to cover with Stucco-Paper, to place my Niche-chimney Piece from my Summer house at one End of it, over that Mr Pope's Busto, &, on each side, my Books. The Windows open into my principal Prospect.' He was also able to achieve a drawing-room or library, of a good size, which he expected to prove 'one of the

Pleasantest Rooms I shall have'. So it may be presumed that he solved the problems humorously presented in a letter to Lady Luxborough on 6 June 1749, in which he described the walls, floors, windows, ceilings, furniture, and pictures as being violently at cross-purposes, and as quarrelling noisily and continuously with him and among themselves. And though he complained that his house was a 'bottomless Pit,... or rather it is a *whirlpool*, which sucks in all my money & that so *deep* that there is not the least glimpse of it appears thro' the water', yet it managed to attract large numbers of guests who uniformly praised its refinement. On 10 September 1748 he entertained to dinner Lady Luxborough, a Captain Outing, a friend of them both, Parson Hall, an old schoolfellow, Lord Dudley of Halesowen Grange, and his sister Miss Lea, Counsellor Corbet, a young barrister, Mr Sanders, an apothecary of Stourbridge, the Rev. John Perry, vicar of Clent, and his wife, and his own cousin Miss Dolman; in addition half a dozen footmen and his own servants and labourers had to be cared for—altogether a very representative selection of the society which revolved round him. Later, the names include some of greater eminence— Thomas Warton, Joseph Spence, who wrote the *Anecdotes*, Home the author of *Douglas*, Thomas Percy, and so on. 'Thus', remarks the poet, 'my *ferme ornée* procures me interviews with persons whom it might otherwise be my *wish*, rather than my good fortune to see' (30 May 1758). Lord Stamford, of Enville, called early in 1750, and 'was much struck

[79]

with Virgil's Grove...gave it the Preference to the
Rock work &c. at Hagley, & said obliging Things'.
The impression, despite a wet day and poor season,
was so favourable that Lord Stamford later sought
Shenstone's counsel about his own estate.

From time to time, however, in spite of this
increasing eminence in the eyes of the world, he
suffers from depression, generally accompanying ill
health, sometimes merely reflecting his annoyance
at the narrowness of his circumstances. He is 'utterly
dissatisfied' (1741), plagued by a bad appetite,
indigestion, sleeplessness, and weak nerves (this even
in the summer time, July 1743), affected by the gloom
of autumn and the dreariness of winter year after
year, and frequently incapacitated by indolence. It
is useless to speculate on his constitution; a neuras-
thenic disorder kept him from sleep, prevented clear
thought and decision, tortured his nerves, and
depressed him. He writes to Jago, in July 1743, that
he is 'much out of order....My vertigo has not *yet*
taken away my senses; God knows how soon it may
do; but my nerves are in such a condition, that I can
scarce get a wink of even *disordered* rest for whole
nights together. May you never know the misery of
such involuntary vigils.' In 1747 he complains of
'bad health, bad spirits, no company to my mind';
in 1751, of 'nervous disorders...nervous fevers....
I am far from well'; in 1757 he finds his head 'so
terribly confused, that it has been with difficulty I
could *think* or *express* myself on the most superficial
topic'; in 1758 he suffers from a 'hypochondriacal'

fever, which leaves his nerves so disturbed that 'even on no very interesting subject, I could readily think myself into a vertigo'. This sounds like a well-known complaint; and sure enough in 1762 he is found suffering from that deplorable importation, which was first noticed in England in 1743, and to which Mrs Montagu referred as 'the fashionable cold called l'influenza'. If Shenstone, with a naturally susceptible constitution, was exposed to this scourge very often, it would readily explain at least some of his periods of depression.

There is no satisfactory explanation of eighteenth-century melancholia. That much of it was nothing but auto-suggestion is unquestionable, particularly in the case of sufferers like Boswell. That a degree might be due to poetic frustration as Arnold suggested in the case of Gray is probable. Perhaps the existence of a healthy poetic tradition, by encouraging the original as opposed to the conventional qualities of his verse, would have helped Shenstone against his lethargy. A healthy poetic interchange might have provided an alternative to an empty leisure, and enabled him to defy his initial constitutional handicap. To Jago, on 11 September 1748, he writes deploring his lethargy: 'You speak of my dwelling in the Castle of Indolence, and I verily believe I *do*. There is something like enchantment in my present inactivity; for without any kind of lett or impediment to the correction of my trifles that I see, I am in no wise able to make the least advances.' And to Lady Luxborough the next year (3 June) he remarked:

'I lead here the unhappy Life of seeing nothing in the Creation half so idle as myself.' It needed considerable courage to publish anything slightly divergent from the convention, as the reaction to Gray's *Odes* proved; and Shenstone—who need hardly have feared on this score—was not in any case seeking publicity. Depression drove him to the 'few friends prejudiced in my favour', and away from the vulgar. In November 1762, he discussed with Graves the prospects of promoting an edition of his poems by subscription. 'When I am low-spirited', he wrote, 'I almost shudder at this tremendous contract with the publick.' As a result, he was very dependent on the support of his friends. To Jago, on one occasion, he even utters the warning, that 'though I could bear the *disregard* of the town, I could not bear to see my friends alter their opinion, which they say they have, of what I write' (January–April 1742). To Graves he expresses his fastidiousness—'one would chuse to please a few *friends* of taste before mob or gentry, the great vulgar or the small' (21 September 1747). And even while prophesying to Jago, in 1750, that the summer would no doubt increase his circle of acquaintance, he reflects that the circle of friends with which he can feel at ease will remain as narrow as ever.

The death of his friends, therefore, naturally affected him deeply. William Somerville, author of *The Chase* and *Field Sports*, was the first to go, in 1742, though the loss was alleviated because he was an old man and rather an acquaintance than a friend.

The death of James Thomson, on 27 August 1748, was more distressing; though Shenstone had known him only two years, he felt the intimacy of a warm friendship, and commemorated it by erecting an urn in Virgil's Grove. 'God knows', he wrote to Jago on this occasion, 'I lean on a very few friends; and if they drop me, I become a wretched misanthrope.' Three years later, in November 1751, his brother Joseph died, and Shenstone was afflicted with the deepest grief; months afterwards he wrote to Graves expressing his continued sense of loss, and ending with the request for sympathy: 'Amongst all changes and chances, I often think of you; and pray there may be no suspicion or jealousy betwixt us during the rest of our lives.' Anthony Whistler died on 10 May 1754, and again Shenstone was plunged into profound gloom, and again wrote for Graves's sympathy: 'Poor Mr Whistler! not a single acquaintance have I made, not a single picture or curiosity have I purchased, not a single embellishment have I given to my place, since he was last here, but I have had his approbation and his amusement in my eye. I will assuredly inscribe my larger urn to his memory; nor shall I pass it without a pleasing melancholy during the remainder of my days....Adieu! my dear friend! may our remembrance of the person we have lost be the strong and everlasting cement of our affection!' A final blow in 1756 robbed him of Lady Luxborough, to whom he had written his liveliest and most entertaining letters. Fortunately Jago outlived him by eighteen years and Graves, as befitted one of his brisk and sanguine condition, survived to a hale old age, actually publishing, just before he died in 1804, a work entitled, *The Invalid; with the Obvious Means of enjoying Health and Long Life, by a Nonagenarian*. And Shenstone was able to some extent to replace his lost friends with new ones. There was a young clergyman named John Pixell, who, born in 1725, had gone up to Queen's College, Oxford, and made a name for himself as a musician. Shenstone first met him in the summer of 1749, when Pixell 'gave me an opportunity of being acquainted with him by frequently visiting, and introducing company to, my walks'. He was an accomplished performer on the violin and harpsichord, and set songs to music, was vicar of Edgbaston from 1750 to 1784, and on one occasion in 1750 'made an agreement with his club at Birmingham, to give me a day's music in some part of my walks'. There was also John Scott Hylton, a pleasant and cultured companion who occupied Lapall House in the parish of Halesowen from 1753 onwards, and in 1784 edited the poems of Richard Jago. More eminent were Thomas Percy and Robert Dodsley and 'my neighbour Baskerville' the printer. (It is a coincidence that Caslon, the famous type-designer, was born at Halesowen in 1692.) Shenstone had long known Humphrey Pitt of Shiffnal, in whose house Percy rescued the famous folio of ballads which was being used by the servants as waste paper, and struck up a warm friendship with Percy as soon as the latter mentioned the ballads to him, late in 1757. Life at The Leasowes, therefore,

[84]

though at times it might cause him dissatisfaction, was sufficiently varied to represent most sides of the cultured interests of the century.

The house itself was replaced after Shenstone's death by a more commodious structure, a quietly gracious square building with Venetian windows, fronting on to the garden and linked to wings of the same character. But in Shenstone's time it was smaller; he drew a picture of it in 1744, showing a farm-house with two gables side by side, above irregularly grouped square-headed windows under square dripstones. There is a small door underneath the gulley of the roof. Later he added a simple square wing to the original building, with a rather lop-sided and incongruous effect, but with added convenience. An eighteenth-century print shows the whole embowered in trees, except in front where it opens to a field with cattle, whence the ground slopes sharply to a belt of trees and the lake. On a knoll overlooking the water Shenstone built the Priory ruin. This retreat was looked upon by contemporaries as an escape from the business of mankind, and so, to some extent, in the absence of good communications, it was. But eighteenth-century rusticity rarely loses its humanity, and there is about The Leasowes a well-bred charm, a gentlemanly elegance, which the period recognized as akin to itself.

To approach it through the eyes of its own century is to sense a new experience, which could find in a few acres of gently cherished landscape a wonderland which attracted statesmen and divines, nobility and commonalty. There was felt in some way to be something momentous about it, and several minute descriptions have survived of this novelty which in a quiet way Georgian England took to its heart, and which is perhaps a symbol of its literate culture—conservatively progressive, hesitatingly unconventional, elegantly natural. We may approach with Richard Graves, through his novel *Columella*, and accompany Atticus and Hortensius as they visit their old college fellow. They leave the Birmingham-Halesowen road, cross one field, enter a grove of oaks, reach a small amphitheatre, and see 'the front of a small gothic house, neatly fitted up, embosomed in a thicket of beech and hornbeam, and a variety of elegant shrubs'. This is faithful enough, except for its wide interpretation of 'gothic'. And at once we are faced with his contemporaries' stock epithet for Shenstone—'elegant'—which, discerning his essential tenancy of one room in the eighteenth-century mansion, they applied to him. 'So simple, yet so elegant' (Heely), 'An elegant lawn...elegant inscriptions' (Whately), 'ingenious and elegant gentleman' (Boswell), 'the sentiments of an elegant mind' (Dodsley), 'our most elegant and amiable friend...the consummate elegance of his taste' (Percy)—the agreement is universal, while his gardens, says the Duchess of Somerset, are 'the most perfect model of rural elegance'. His own *Ode to Rural Elegance* struck the note at once. And despite the slightly different meaning of the word, this unanimity is significant.

[86]

Arriving with Atticus and Hortensius, we should expect to find the proprietor, a heavily built man with a large sleepily pleasant face as his portraits show him, reposing gracefully under a tree with a copy of *The Seasons* by his friend Thomson. But we should, in fact, find him running about in a paroxysm of rage caused by some errant pigs which have uprooted a primrose bed. Perhaps this is an indiscreet approach; Columella does not entirely tally with Shenstone, or Graves could not have claimed—and shown—a genuine regard for his friend's memory. Besides, he testifies in the *Recollection*: 'I do not remember ever to have seen him in a passion'. It might be fairer to accompany Geoffry Wildgoose and his henchman Tugwell, in *The Spiritual Quixote*, on their summer's ramble during which they see 'an object amidst the woods which...they were told was Shenstone's Folly'. This appellation has been applied to The Leasowes by the uncomprehending rustics. In the fading sunset they follow a lane, and come upon a gentleman wearing his own hair, which is turning a little grey with middle age, and dressed in a plain blue coat and scarlet waistcoat, with broad gold lace. (The poet, as Graves testifies elsewhere, favoured bright colours in dress.) This is 'the now celebrated Mr Shenstone, whose place began to be frequented by people of distinction from all parts of England on account of its natural beauties which by mere force of genius and good taste Mr Shenstone had improved'. The proprietor courteously displays his cascades, urns, reservoirs, statues, inscriptions,

[87]

and Virgil's Grove, and describes his visitors of quality and taste. We might supply a list of these from Shenstone's letters; they would include, besides the friends already mentioned, William Pitt, himself an enthusiastic gardener, who was so struck with The Leasowes that he offered, through the agency of Sanderson Miller, to lay out £200 himself for their development—an offer which Shenstone austerely turned down. His circle of acquaintance beyond The Leasowes included 'My Friend Burke' in England, and Adam Smith, John Home, author of *Douglas*, and Robertson the historian, in Scotland, all of whom in 1761 send him 'their compliments centuplicated'. His list of visitors for the summer of 1762 is worth transcribing merely for its variety—he offers to Graves to 'particularize a few' of his guests. The list runs: 'the Duke and Dutchess of Richmond—Mr Walsh, Member for Worcester—Earl of Bath with Dr Monson, Mrs Montague (who wrote the three last Dialogues printed with Lord Lyttelton's), and other company, from Hagley—Sir Richard Ashley—Mr Mordaunt—Dr Charlton with Mr Knight—Earl and Countess of Northampton—Mr Amyand—Lord Plymouth and Sir Harry Parker—Mr and Mrs Morrice of Percefield—Lord Mansfield with Mr Baron Smythe, Lord Dartmouth and Mr Talbot—Marquis of Tavistock and Earl of Ossory—your nephew Mr Graves with Mr Hopton and one of the senior Proctors of Oxford—Lord and Lady Dacre—Baron Plessen, Gentleman of the Bed-Chamber to the King of Denmark, with Mr Wendt his Tutor—Lord and

Lady Vernon of Sudbury with his children, Sir Charles and Lady Tynte, and Mr Garrick's brother—Mr and Mrs Melmoth—Colonel James—Lady Ward and Lady Uill, with Miss Wrottesley, Miss Pigott, &c.— Lord Lyttelton, Mr Lyttelton, and Mr Rust—Lord and Lady Dartmouth with Lord and Lady Willoughby de Broke—Mr Anson of Shuckburgh with Mr Stuart the painter and publisher of *Athenian Ruins*—Mr Pepys and Sir W. Wheeler's son, Mr Pitt's nephew, &c.—Colonel Bamfylde with Mr Knight's Family, &c. &c.' Many of these are no longer even *Nominis Umbrae*, but at the time such multifold attention seemed to vindicate Shenstone's chosen course of life. Returning to *The Spiritual Quixote*, we could follow Geoffry Wildgoose into his 'elegant bedchamber fitted up in a Gothic taste; to which the bed itself, the rest of the furniture and the painted glass in the window, all corresponded'; and the next morning we might admire the poet's equanimity when he discovers that his guest, in the name of Methodism and Christian zeal against the idolatrous works of human ambition, has done vigorous and extensive damage to his urns and cascades.

But such a fragmentary visit would reveal little of the beauty which attracted the attentions of taste. Robert Dodsley paid tribute to his friend's memory by adding to his edition of Shenstone's works a *Description of The Leasowes* with a map—a description which powerfully affected the imagination of Sir Walter Scott as a boy. And Dodsley's description was followed by other connoisseurs of the picturesque. Thomas Whately's *Observations on Modern Gardening* are a good example of the writing *con amore* which The Leasowes stimulated. He 'plunges into a dark narrow dell, filled with small trees', sees the brook falling in a series of cascades, and traces it by its sound running among the roots of thickets, admires 'the pretty landscape' towards Halesowen, with its steeple seen in an angle of the hills; notices the gently sloping fields; passes from scene to scene, from grave to gay, from a solitary neglected hollow overrun with bushes and fern, which receives a rill issuing in a cascade from a thicket of alder and hornbeam, to the 'animated scene' where the fall is to be seen through the branches of the trees with the sunlight playing on it in patches. He then ascends from the hollow, reaches the brow of the hill and looks down across the tops of the trees from which he has emerged, over to the cheerful cornfields of the opposite slope; he crosses the fields in front of the house and admires the 'prospect...of endless variety', a brisk extensive scene of prosperous country all the way from Halesowen to the Wrekin, thirty miles distant. And as the century demanded variety in its landscape, here was God's plenty. The slender resources of The Leasowes were utilized so as to provide a new sensation at every turn. 'The variety...is wonderful; all the enclosures are totally different; there is seldom a single circumstance in which they agree.' So he passes from his 'elevated gay situation' to the quiet pasture and lawn before the house, and then descends again to a 'little waste', 'shut up by rude trees' and 'wild hanging coppices' where he finds among the great trees a small irregular lake, enlivened by the shafts of light which break between them, where the stillness and reflections arouse a pleasing meditation. The next transition is by the ascent of the hill to the straight walk—which (a sign of the times) by the mere fact of its straightness he finds 'too artificial for The Leasowes'—and thence he descends again by the fields through 'varieties of ground, enclosures, hedges, thickets', past haystacks and round the end of the slope on top of which there stands the house—a pastoral progress which would have delighted the heart of Batty Langley. The final scene is a climax; a synopsis in Alfred Jingle's manner is the only way of conveying the excitement with which the visitor approached Virgil's Grove. It would run as follows (the component expressions being Whately's own): 'End of path—enchanting grove—small valley—lovely rivulet—precipitate cascade—seen through trees—glittering at a distance—everywhere clear dappled by gleams of light—shadow of leaves on water—verdure of foliage, grass, trees—stately forest trees in groups —valley descends—gloomy—rivulet lost in pool— large trees—bridge—simple to rudeness—solemnity —small obelisk—genius of Virgil—delightful spot.' And here, adjoining the Priory Walk where he had entered, the visitor completed the circle, and knew what a *ferme ornée* was like.

The mere catalogue of sights which the traveller

charts is enough to exhaust the imagination. We are quite ready to agree with his conclusion, 'that every natural advantage of the place has been discovered, applied, contrasted, and carried to the utmost perfection, in the purest taste, and with inexhaustible fancy'. When the same impression is repeated by one visitor after another, one begins to feel that in The Leasowes the century found a satisfactory crystallization of those ideals of human association, elegiac naturalism, well-bred charm and variety, with a touch of the dramatic, which it was formulating for itself as it progressed.

Joseph Heely, in his *Letters on the Beauties of...
The Leasowes*, is inspired to the same enthusiasm. He quotes Milton on his title-page—

> For Nature here
> Wantons as in her prime, and plays at will
> Her virgin fancies—

and he congratulates his countrymen on the emergence of gardening from that 'vicious and puerile state' which prevailed when Le Nôtre walked around 'eternally fondling the rule and the line, those baneful instruments'. The landscape is 'so simple, yet so elegant; every scene so beautifully characterized; so different, yet so configurative'. The writing stirs with an undercurrent of excitement as he enters 'the steep gloomy glen covered with trees' which was the introduction to The Leasowes, and passes by the Priory arch and the Priory walk into a quiet sequestered valley where 'the superlative genius of Shenstone stood confessed on every object'.

Here is the cascade, 'in the very image of nature herself'; there are the shelving rocks and huge massy stones, the entangled thickets and sudden declivities worthy of a Salvator; here is a 'pensive sombrous valley' studded with umbrageous trees; there is the lively verdure of the turf variegated with the hues of different field flowers. He sees the current, stealing smoothly along the bottom, or checked by little falls, gurgling among the stones. And his sensations become at times quite bacchanal—'a little enthusiasm if it hang not about you should be courted for the more perfect enjoyment of such classic ground'. For his own part, he confesses, 'I could not, for the soul of me, help thinking myself surrounded, as my eyes glanced over the woody scene, by those imaginary beings whom fable gives life to, skipping about me in wanton revelry'. For the eighteenth century, in fact, The Leasowes combined the attractions of Arcadia, the Vale of Tempe, Nymphidia, Claude Lorrain, Gaspar Poussin, and Salvator Rosa. And even after the passage of almost a hundred years, an American visitor Hugh Miller, writing his *First Impressions of England and its People*, though he joined Graves and Goldsmith (Essay XXI of *Essays...in 1765*) in a *sic transit*, praised it for its varied charm and artistic delicacy, and witnessed to its attractions for anyone 'who can see spirit and genius even in a vignette, beauty in the grouping of a clump, in the sweep of a knoll, in the convexity of a mossy bank, in the glitter of a half-hidden stream, or the blue gleam of a solitary lochan'.

The theories which partly dictated and partly resulted from Shenstone's practice comprise his *Unconnected Thoughts on Gardening* included in *Men and Manners*, that collection of *pensées* for which by temperament he was so well fitted. The original components of Sharawadgi have been defined as a distaste for the geometrical, a flair for variety and irregularity, and a respect for Nature's potential design. Involved in these, too, there was the idea that the aesthetics of landscape were identical with those of pictorial art.

By these standards, Shenstone would have gratified the Chinese as well as he charmed his countrymen. He found himself unable to understand the former taste for straight lines: there is no joy in a garden where 'the foot is to travel over what the eye has done before'. When pattern is to be viewed in a *coup d'œil*, there is an excuse for geometry; but when the spectator is forced to advance through a nature where the smallest detail is methodized, his progress is slow to the point of dulness. Shenstone will admit no virtues in regular pattern, involving as it does an identity achieved at the expense of Nature, and of 'that variety which the natural country supplies everywhere'.

'That variety'—we remember that Hogarth's *Analysis*, burning incense to the 'waving line, or line of beauty', bore on its title-page a device like an eel standing on its tail within a pyramid, above the sacred motto, 'Variety'. It is variety which pleases in a ruin, the variety and irregularity of surface,

which contrasts scenes and defines them against one
another, which keeps the mind in a liveliness of
expectation, which justifies the introduction of the
peasant's cottage, which insists that water should
only appear 'as an irregular lake or winding stream'.
In fact, to apply the pictorial criterion, as Shenstone
wrote, 'landskip should contain variety enough to
form a picture upon canvas: and this is no bad test,
as I think the landskip painter is the gardiner's best
designer'. Yet variety is not anarchy; the balance is
preserved as the painter preserves it, not by the
symmetry of identical masses, but by subtler means
of sharing the eye's interest equally between the two
sides of a composition.

And as for Nature's potential design, that is the
very foundation of Art. 'Ground should first be
considered with an eye to its peculiar character:
whether it be the grand, the savage, the sprightly,
the melancholy, the horrid, or the beautifull.' Its
shape, the appropriate growth of trees, and the disposition of water, things particularly dictated by
natural law, are correspondingly sacred. For Shenstone is aware, like his enlightened contemporaries,
that Nature is not the realm of chance. If it sometimes seems so to us, that is because we have limited
faculties—'endued neither with organs, nor allowed
a station, proper to give us an universal view; or to
exhibit to us the variety, the orderly proportions, and
dispositions of the system.' Man, therefore, humbly
admits his partial views. Yet he cannot rest there;
Art is 'often requisite to collect and epitomize the

beauties of nature', and human skill is to be used after the Aristotelean precept for the perfection of natural beauty. The beauty which was no doubt to be seen in the universe as a whole, were one's faculties divinely comprehensive, might be achieved in miniature by a discreet manipulation. But it was therefore all the more important that man should serve, and not thwart, Nature. 'Why fantastically endeavor to humanize those vegetables, of which nature, discreet nature, thought it proper to make trees? Why endow the vegetable bird with wings, which nature has made momentarily dependent upon the soil?' From complaints like these, it seems that current taste had progressed very little since the time when Addison, forty years before, had made his protest. The accusations, the tone, even (suspiciously) the phrasing, are practically the same. There is the citizen who plants his trees in rows, clips his yews, displays his water in fountains, 'in short, admires no part of nature but her ductility; exhibits every thing that is glaring, that implies expence, or that effects a surprize because it is unnatural'. Perhaps this is conventional satire, drawn, like much of the social criticism of the century, by uncontaminated conduits from the fountain-head of Addison; perhaps it is the reflection of a grievous aesthetic lag on the part of the bourgeoisie. If the latter were the case, the bourgeois showed great agility during the next few years. Complaints against his geometrical gardens give way without warning to protests against the undisciplined wildness of his new fancy. *The World*, on

12 April 1753, remarked how far the rage for improvement had spread—would that our own popular periodicals were so outspoken. The 'vast multitude of grotesque little villas which grow up every summer within a certain distance of London', remarked *The World*, are 'fatal proofs of the degeneracy of our national taste'. Degeneracy? Because of an intoxication with geometry? Not by any means. The new style demands spires, gargoyles, stucco, battlements, suits of armour, temples to Venus, bridges 'partly in the Chinese manner'. This is four years before Sir William Chambers gave chinoiserie the eminent assistance of his *Designs for Chinese Buildings*, and nearly twenty before his famous *Dissertation on Oriental Gardening* claimed for that art among the Chinese an effect only comparable with that of music on the Greeks. (The Chinese, declared Chambers, respect gardening so highly that they say that its efficacy in moving the passions compares well with that of any other art whatever, while their gardeners —perhaps this is a cut at the humble 'Capability' Brown, who was anathema to Chambers—are 'also Painters and Philosophers'.) The citizen's intentions, as always, were of the best; he was as willing to adopt the Chinese in the interests of good taste as he is to-day to embrace the Tudor. The results were nearly as strange. *On croyait imiter la nature, et on ne faisait que la singer.* William Mason was moved to address outraged Nature as follows:

> Let those who, weekly, from the city's smoke
> Croud to each neighb'ring hamlet, there to hold

Their dusty sabbath, tip with gold and red
The milk-white palisades, that Gothic now,
And now Chinese, now neither, and yet both,
Chequer their trim domain. Thy sylvan scene
Would fade indignant at the tawdry glare.

We may suppose that Shenstone would not approve
the 'grove perplexed with errors and crooked walks',
the 'labyrinth of hornbeam hedges', the mazes and
open spaces and flowers and fountains mixed together
which cause *The World* so much pain. The bourgeois
was making up for lost time—and was still accused
of degeneracy. *Plus ça change....*

Shenstone's naturalistic views were helped, rather
ironically, by that very slenderness of purse which
caused him such exasperation. He was forced to
rely on his own designs rather than on those of a
doctrinaire professional, and to utilize all the help
that Nature could afford him. There is nothing about
The Leasowes to rival Kent's dead tree, or the truly
Herculean energies of the gentleman in Holcroft's
Anna St Ives, who complains: 'I have the wilderness
very much at heart, but the soil is so excellent, and
I scarcely know how we shall make the land sufficiently barren. I have planted one year, and grubbed
up the next; built and pulled down; dug and filled
up again; removed hills, and sent them back to their
old stations; and all from a determination to do
whatever could be done. And now I believe there
are no grounds in all England so wooded and shut-in,
as those of Wenbourne Hill, notwithstanding its
situation on a very commanding eminence. We are

surrounded by coppices, groves, espaliers, and plantations.' Shenstone had to be humbler. The formation of Virgil's Grove, the first improvement, was effected by husbanding the limited water-supply so that a cascade might result from a careful combination of trickles. Gilpin, who found The Leasowes 'whimsical but amusing', nevertheless disapproved of its streams; they were not vigorous enough to keep themselves clean, and he thought it ridiculous to see the Naiads invited to bathe their limbs in the crystal floods, if the crystal floods themselves needed dredging. But if a scanty income had drawbacks, it enforced careful thought. The problem of achieving perfection with small means was a discipline. 'Fondness for mere concetto' was as much beyond Shenstone's power as it was beyond his desire. Nature itself had to be treated, not as raw material waiting for man to impose his pattern on it, but in itself as potential pattern, waiting merely to be clarified.

As befitted the eighteenth century, it was a pattern in relation to man. The hamlets brown and dim-discovered spires are an essential component of the century's landscapes. Church steeples, said Gilbert White, 'are very necessary ingredients in an elegant landscape'. A hermit might be a hermit, but he would expect visitors. A retreat might be a retreat, but all its vistas would be designed to display the clustering houses of the nearest village. From The Leasowes, the eye travelled down the slope, over the ruined Priory, to the cottages and slender spire of Halesowen, and beyond that to where the Lyttelton's sham castle caught the attention on the sky-line, below the peak of Clent hill.

Remembering that the relation between Nature and man was a co-operation and not a rivalry, the place of human handiwork in The Leasowes is easily understood. Shenstone has been blamed for proclaiming his fidelity to Nature, and then admitting classical urns and Gothic screens. They were, however, the punctuation marks by which the grammar of natural meaning was regulated. They formed focal points of interest, gave distinction between one scene and another, and deepened the particular communication of each component.

The kind of definition in most cases is pretty evident. Shenstone reflects, for example, on the appeal of literary or historical associations: 'What an advantage must some Italian seats derive from the circumstance of being situate on ground mentioned in the classicks? And even in England, wherever a park or garden happens to have been the scene of any event in history, one would surely avail one's self of that circumstance, to make it more interesting to the imagination.' This literary fallacy had a powerful effect. One thinks of Virgil's Grove. The dedication implied a particular mood which half-prepared the visitor for the qualities of the place before he reached it. And when friends died, they could be commemorated there with urns which aroused a 'pleasing melancholy'. Just as the vogue for Claude was probably increased by the nostalgia for classic scenes which appealed to the Italy-loving

Englishman, so it is not fantastic to feel in the urns
and inscriptions of The Leasowes, and of similar
gardens which wove the artificial into the natural,
the mood of the ancient desiderium, the longing for
what has irrecoverably departed—that mood of
which perhaps the classical expression in English is
that passage in Landor's imaginary conversation
between Aesop and Rhodope beginning 'Helen died,
Laodameia died, Leda the beloved of Jupiter went
before', and ending 'there is no name, with whatever
emphasis of passionate love repeated, of which the
echo is not faint at last'. It is appropriate to recall
that of the epitaph which Shenstone wrote for his
cousin Maria Dolman, who died suddenly in 1753,
Landor said that it was the finest he knew.

> Ah Maria
> Puellarum elegantissima,
> Ah flore venustatis abrepta,
> Vale!
> Heu quanto minus est
> Cum reliquis versari,
> Quam tui
> Meminisse!

Whoever should study the mood of desiderium in
England during the eighteenth century might find
corroboration for the sense of restrained poignancy
which often underlies the good poetry of the age—
a poignancy sometimes obliterated from our gaze by
the more visible violence of the Romantic Revival;
at any rate, as Sir Thomas Browne would say, he
should not fall on trite or trivial disquisitions.

[101]

Nature and man did not exist apart from each other. Shenstone, supposed to be a recluse, reminds us of the Alexander Selkirk of Cowper's poem when he is deprived of society. Gray's *Elegy*, as Mr Empson has pointed out, owes much of the perfection of its feeling to that harmonious union which associates the life of man with the greater rhythms of seasonal change, makes his pilgrimage more serious and momentous, and at the same time so universalizes his transience that it soothes into a calm melancholy our reactions of practical pity. If the Romantics were to bring man and Nature into a union, it had to be by the spiritualization of both:

> Cuckoo, shall I call thee bird,
> Or but a wandering voice?

Coleridge believed that it is insufficient to produce 'images, however beautiful, though faithfully copied from nature, and as accurately represented in words', unless at the same time 'a human and intellectual life is transferred to them from the poet's own spirit'. Wordsworth's daffodils are not earthly, nor are the nightingale and the cuckoo of *The Solitary Reaper*, nor the albatross of Coleridge, nor Shelley's skylark and cloud and west wind. Wordsworth feels that he cannot look at Nature properly unless it be through a glory and a dream, that the meanest flower arouses thoughts too deep for tears. We can imagine Dr Johnson's comment: 'Sir, if it made me such a fool, I should never look at it'. The eighteenth century sometimes spiritualized the country: Akenside did so in his *Pleasures of the Imagination*, Collins in the *Ode to Evening*, Thomson in his appeals to the

> Source of Being! Universal Soul
> Of heaven and earth!

And Gray's *Odes* recall the warmly coloured allegories of Nicholas—not Gaspar—Poussin. But there are other attitudes equally significant—quite apart from the bastard pastoral and the bastard 'romantick' derived from Spenser and Milton. The two which most symbolize the interests of the century are, I think, the desire for a rural retreat, and the careful love of natural history.

> A farm some twenty miles from town,
> Small, tight, salubrious, and my own;
> A pond before, full to the brim,
> Where cows may cool, and geese may swim:
> Behind, a green like velvet neat,
> Soft to the eye, and to the feet,
> Where od'rous plants in evening fair
> Breathe all around ambrosial air.

That is from Matthew Green's *Cure for the Spleen*, and it has numerous counterparts throughout the century—Pope's *Ode to Solitude*, the Countess of Winchilsea's *Petition for an Absolute Retreat*, Parnell's *Hymn to Contentment*, and Rogers' *A Wish*, to take a few. It expresses a cheerful and sensible love of Nature, neither mystical nor mysterious, and very normal in the century even when, as in Goldsmith's *Deserted Village*, it is coloured by roseate

[103]

reminiscence. Related to it, though often vitiated by poetic diction, is the desire to describe Nature honestly, fixing on the object the eye of the mind if not of the body. The Countess of Winchilsea's *Nocturnal Reverie*, parts of Pope's *Windsor Forest*, much of *The Seasons* (especially its admirable vignettes), Somerville's *Chase* and other poems of country life, Cowper's *Task*, Dyer's *Grongar Hill*, even a great part of works which, like *The Fleece*, valiantly try to conquer for poetry realms which look so unpromising, share this faithfulness to natural history. They go for the fact, rather than the spirituality, of things, and are content with images faithfully copied from nature and accurately represented in words. It is interesting to find the same virtues in prose, in those numerous excellent individuals who observed and noted, leading the way to Gilbert White. Shenstone, though not a naturalist, gives one this sort of feeling; his love for the country-side depends on its 'pleasing employment', the joy of noticing flowers and shrubs, untroubled by mystic intuitions, content to be amused and interested by the behaviour of the farm-yard, the harvesting of a hayfield, or the gambols of a rivulet.

But in his more reflective moments it was a different satisfaction he sought, one to be supplied rather by the artificial-natural of the garden, which could become a vehicle for literary moods. And therefore he remembered Whistler in one corner, Somerville in another, and Thomson in another, and when he dedicated a seat to Jago, a second to Graves, and a third to Percy, when the procession of epitaphs passed before him, he could combine the liberating effect of natural scenery with the recollection of past or present friendships, and catch a flavour of melancholy which, in its luxurious palatableness, belonged particularly to his generation.

PART IV

AUREA MEDIOCRITAS

Rectius vives, Licini, neque altum
semper urgendo neque, dum procellas
cautus horrescis, nimium premendo
    litus iniquum.

    .   .   .   .   .

saepius ventis agitatur ingens
pinus et celsae graviore casu
decidunt turres feriuntque summos
    fulgura montes.   HORACE

Here, undisturbed by the noise of the world's conflicts, unmoved by the vicissitudes of party or sect,
Shenstone passed his life. 'I keep no political
company, nor desire any', he had written to Graves,
in 1742. In *Men and Manners* he counselled against
party extremism, and in the last of his letters that
has survived, written on 16 January 1763, within a
month of his death, he repeated the same sentiment
to Percy: 'I profess to no Party but moderation'.
Echoes of the '45 broke for a short while the usual
quietness of Halesowen, and set country squires,
workmen, and rustics, comparing the House of Stuart
with that of Hanover, and apprehending the advent
of Popery; and a final rumble from the affair filled
a letter to Graves late in 1746, when the Lords
Kilmarnock and Balmerino were executed. But

there are not many political references; news came slowly, sometimes through the Lytteltons, sometimes through Lady Luxborough's friend Sir William Meredith, and often, no doubt, through his visitors and the various magazines and reviews. He often felt starved for information: 'as to what passes in the busy world', he tells Graves on 1 March 1761, 'I know no more than the *Chronicle* informs me—unless *your* letters happen to be *rounded* with little anecdotes from Bath.' At times he paid visits and varied the circle of country life with friendly calls on his neighbours, on one of which, 'what with wine, sitting up late, a perfect flux of discourse, and a return home through the dark', he found himself, as he euphemistically puts it, '*vertiginous* before I was aware', and spent the next day abhorring himself in dust and ashes. Expeditions to Lady Luxborough's 'perfect Arcadia' at Barrels provided an opportunity for cultured discussions on poetry and gardening. At other times he repaid the visits made to him by Lord Stamford of Enville, and in 1758 attended the Worcester music meeting with the natural excitement of one who 'has not seen a public place these ten years'. Here he was able to hear *The Messiah* and to pronounce it the finest of Handel's works, though not without occasional blemishes.

The lives of the coterie which circled round him constitute a very faithful picture of the society of the mid-century, though Horace Walpole for some strange reason characterized them to Cole as 'puny conceited witlings who give themselves airs from being in possession of the soil of Parnassus for the time being' (27 April 1773). (Shenstone himself appropriately summed Walpole up as 'a lively and ingenious writer; not always accurate in his determinations, and much less so in his language'.) There was a cheerful Anglican sobriety in Jago and Graves; contact with the world of books, in Robert Dodsley, John Baskerville, Thomas Percy, and the continual flow of friendly authors who visited The Leasowes; the excitement of politics, in Lord Lyttelton; the benevolent rural oligarchy, in Lady Luxborough. It is the cultured society of the century, gossiping about its own poems or the latest publications of Gray or Fielding or Smollett, and in the meantime setting obelisks on points of vantage, or diverting a stream. The Duchess of Somerset, on 15 May 1748, wrote a charming description of her country occupations to her friend Lady Luxborough: 'A Piece of waste Ground, on the lower Side of the Abbey-Walk, has been turned into a Corn-Field, and a Turf-Walk, about eight Feet wide, round it: close to a flourishing Hawthorn Hedge; on one Side, there is a thatched Seat open on three Sides, which pretends to no Name of greater Dignity, than justly belongs to what it represents, namely a Shepherd's Hut; before it there is an irregular Piece of Turf, which was spared for the Sake of some old Oaks and Beeches, which are scattered upon it: and as you are sitting down there, you have, under these Boughs, a direct View of *Windsor* Castle. There are Sweet-Williams, Narcissus's, Rose-Campions, and such Flowers as the

Hares will not eat, in little Borders, round the Foot of every Tree: and I almost flatter myself, that you would not be displeased with the rural Appearance of the whole. The Rains have given us the strongest Verdure I ever saw; our Lawns and Meadows are enamelled with a Profusion of Dasies and Cowslips, and we have the greatest Appearance of Fruit that has been seen these many Years.'

Shenstone frequently found life no less pleasant. 'I saunter about my grounds, take snuff, and read *Clarissa*.' To Christopher Wren of Wroxhall Abbey (a grandson of the architect) he enumerates his diversions on 22 July 1752: 'I neither read nor write aught besides a few letters; and I give myself up entirely to scenes of dissipation; lounge at my Lord Dudley's for near a week together; make dinners; accept of invitations; sit up till three o'clock in the morning with young sprightly married women, over white port and *vin de paysans*; ramble over my fields; issue out orders to my hay-makers; foretel rain and fair weather; enjoy the fragrance of hay, the cocks, and the wind-rows; admire that universal lawn, which is produced by the scythe; sometimes inspect, and draw mouldings for my carpenters; sometimes paper my walls, and at other times my cielings; do every social office that falls in my way, but never seek out for any.' This particular burst of enjoyment, it is true, was an attempt to overcome too painful memories of his brother's recent death; Shenstone rarely enjoyed pleasure unalloyed with pain, and looked on the two sensations as inseparably bound together, so that the prospect of the one was always tempering the presence of the other. Autumn reminded him mournfully of the approach of winter, and winter was relieved by the expectation of spring.

The correspondence with his friends is full of references to their common interests. 'Not a Moment of my Time passes', he tells Dodsley, 'but I am employed, either in overseeing Labourers; reading Robinson's [*sic*] *History of Scotland*; writing in my Paper Books, ('tis not material *what*, but writing;) perplexing the *Birmingham* Artists with Sketches for Improvements in their Manufactures, which they *will* not understand; and lastly, and finally, feeding my Poultry, my Ducks, my Pigeons, and my Swans.' He promotes a subscription to add a couple of bells to the six which the parish church already possesses; rejoices in his accomplishments as a virtuoso in miniature, collecting coins and medals; plays the harpsichord, practises singing, and takes up flower-painting; discusses the opening of an avenue or the proportions of an urn. Lady Luxborough inquires about papier-mâché decorations for her room, which are sold by a Mr Bromwich, at the Golden Lion on Ludgate Hill; Shenstone advises her to buy 'an Ornament for the Middle, and four Spandrells for the Corners' and goes to the trouble of taking an ornamental pineapple from his own ceiling as a sample. He instructs her how to design a shrubbery walk and a plantation of abeles, 'to plant here & there a Yew-tree...to look wild', to plan 'the Sweep

[111]

for the Coach', and proposes haystacks in the form of pyramids to improve the appearance of her grounds. There are fewer references to his own improvements during the later years of his occupancy, but he constructs two little islands in the stream in Virgil's Grove, and is occupied all the summer of 1760 with 'one Piece of water below my Priory'. Dodsley presents him with his portrait, painted by Reynolds; Shenstone's own portrait, by Alcock, provides some excitement in February 1760, when he asks Graves: 'What think you of a tawney or reddish brown for the robe or night-gown, with black for the waist-coat and breeches...?' He acts as a Maecenas to James Woodhouse, the poetical cobbler —'a young journey-man shoe-maker...that lives at the village of Rowley, near me'—of whom Johnson truly remarked that he might prove an excellent shoe-maker, but could never be a good poet. And he rejoices in the visits of his friends; of the Lyttel-tons, and their cousin Admiral Temple West, second-in-command at the engagement for which Byng was executed, and who, though completely exonerated, died in 1758 from the shock of his commander's death; of Dodsley; and of Percy, who stayed at The Leasowes at the end of 1762, not in the least realizing that it would be his last visit to the owner.

Literature shared with gardening the greater part of his interests. His letters are full of references to contemporary publications; to *The Castle of Indolence*, which—surpassing Bentley's judgment on Pope's *Homer*—he thought 'a very pretty Poem, & also a good imitation of Spenser'; to Fielding, whose *Joseph Andrews* he unaccountably found tedious, but whose *Tom Jones* made him laugh at a time when he feared to lose that faculty through disuse. *Clarissa* was prolix; *Grandison* inferior to it, though nevertheless he considered that Richardson deserved a bishopric merely on the strength of it—a tribute perhaps more equivocal than he intended. The *Elegy Written in a Country Churchyard*, at that time anonymous, he liked 'too well', probably thinking how it threw his own elegies into the shade; he cast a critical eye upon Walpole's *Anecdotes of Painting* and remarked, of the author's enthusiasm for the past, 'I never knew so much Genius as Walpole's in such a Bigot to Antiquity.' For Johnson he had a deep respect, and upon the report that his *Shakespeare* would be published during the winter of 1757–8 he expressed the hope to Percy that 'the world may recompence him for a Degree of Industry very seldom connected with so much real Genius'. He came in contact with Johnson at one remove through Percy, who was a friend of both men, and Johnson sent him a poem called *The Parish Clerk* by Vernon (a private soldier in the Buffs), which included a compliment on *The Schoolmistress*. This was in the summer of 1759; in February 1760 he praises *The Rambler* highly to Graves, and the following August thanks Johnson, through Percy, for some expression of regard: 'I do very unfeignedly respect both the Writer & the Man, and should be sorry to forfeit, by a neglect on my side, any degree of esteem he discovers for Me.'

The most important literary activity of his later years, however, was connected not with contemporary but with ancient literature. Thomas Percy had, at some time, procured the folio of ballads from Humphrey Pitt, and he mentioned it to Shenstone in a letter on 24 November 1757. Johnson had already been informed about it and desired publication. More than that, he had expressed a willingness to assist, even to add notes drawn from his wide experience of literature in general and lexicography in particular. Shenstone wrote to Percy, on 4 January 1758, full of excitement; he suggested that the manuscript should be considered as 'an hoard of gold, somewhat defac'd by Time', and proposed to Percy to draw extracts from it on occasion and present them to the world.

But Johnson is wrestling with Shakespeare, and, says Percy, 'has his hands full at present'. The hands, moreover, remain full until 1765, and so, though Johnson may claim the praise of being the original, he is not the only, begetter of the *Reliques*. It was Shenstone who really urged the project forward. The details of the scheme have been presented in full by Mr L. F. Powell (in *The Library* for September 1928) and Mr Irving L. Churchill (in the publications of the Modern Language Association of America, December 1936). At first, while Percy was mainly waiting for Johnson to dispose of Shakespeare, little progress was made; then, in 1759, his own attention was diverted to certain literary activities which he himself had undertaken, a translation from Ovid and another from a Chinese novel, which eventually appeared in four volumes in 1761, as *Hau Kiou Choan; or, The Pleasing History*. Meanwhile, he exchanged transcripts from the ballads with Shenstone, starting by borrowing a copy which the latter possessed of *Gil Morris* for collation with the *Child Maurice* of the Folio. After this, his letters from time to time contained copies of ballads for Shenstone's comment and amusement. In accordance with the poet's original advice to present the ballads to the world 'under more current impressions', the process of editing started. The correspondence frequently refers to 'improvements' bestowed on the rough diamonds of antiquity, and Shenstone expressed himself clearly on 3 February 1762: 'if you publish these old pieces *unimproved only*, I consider them as not every one's money, but as a prize merely for either *virtuosoes*; or else the manufacturers in this kind of ware, The Poets namely.' And in a long letter to John Mac-Gowan, of Edinburgh, Writer to the Signet, on 24 September 1761, Shenstone remarks that Percy has 'offered me a rejecting power, of which I mean to make considerable use'.

It is easy to see the deplorable consequences of such editorial principles, and censure has not failed to fall on both Shenstone and Percy. Some of the 'improvements' are atrocious; all are regrettable. But if we remember how very cautious the mid-century was, how it hesitated to cross the threshold into the new reverence for mediaevalism, we can see how Percy was situated. The eighteenth century did not, on the whole, like editions for specialists. It was not willing to take a great deal of trouble over the reading of poetry, as Johnson proved by his treatment of the metaphysicals and of Gray; and it had been habituated for a hundred years, from the time of Mr Waller and Sir John Denham, to the idea that the sweetness of English verse was never understood or practised by the old poets. The choice, therefore, was clear—either to please the public by making antiquity palatable, as Walpole did at Strawberry Hill, or to satisfy the demands of antiquarian scholarship. We should put the latter aim first; the eighteenth century thought differently. And perhaps if we recall that only very recently have we heard Elizabethan music uncloyed by the harmonies of later improvers, we may realize how slowly the idea has grown that we should let the past speak with its own voice.

Meanwhile Johnson, though too busy to help with textual matters, was smoothing out the business difficulties which Percy encountered. He gave advice when negotiations were in hand with the Dodsleys, and when, despite James Dodsley's acquiescence, Robert proved awkward, he approached Andrew Millar as an alternative publisher. But after what Percy calls 'a council of war with Mr Johnson', on 22 May 1761, the matter of publication was decided, and the Dodsleys bought the book. And finally Johnson, probably while staying with Percy at Easton Maudit in August 1764, assisted in the composition of a dedication to the Countess of Northumberland. So, two years after Shenstone's death, the completed *Reliques* appeared in 1765, and Shenstone, who had done a great deal of work for them, including detailed examination of several previous ballad collections, suggestions for the plan of the whole work, and the enlistment of collaborators like John MacGowan, received his posthumous meed of gratitude in the Preface, and only through a late change of intention on Percy's part failed to find himself the dedicatee of the undertaking.

As for The Leasowes, it is probable that nothing contributed so effectively to give him a sense of power, to subdue his feeling of social inferiority. He tended it like a child, was hungry for praise of it, and, when praise came, thirsted for the credit due to his ingenuity. This eagerness was perhaps sharpened by the fear that Hagley would outshine him, and though Graves declares it absurd to imagine a rivalry between the gentleman's farm and the nobleman's mansion, yet Shenstone was sometimes touchy. Thinking of Thomson's death, he writes to Lady Luxborough that 'he might have found some satisfaction here notwithstanding the vicinity and the Table of H[agley]'. And there is a letter to Sherrington Davenport, of 4 January 1763, previously quoted, about the 'pompous piles of Hagley', and a second of the same date, to Jago, praising certain lines in that gentleman's poem *Labour and Genius*. 'Nothing could be happier than what you say about H[agley]; as it touches in the *gentlest* manner, on a possible truth, which, if expressed rather than implied, might not

be altogether inoffensive.' The lines I presume to be
the following which refer to The Leasowes:

> For sons of Taste, and daughters fair,
> Hasted the sweet delight to share;
> While HAGLEY wondered at their stay,
> And hardly brooked the long delay.

But this is only an occasional petulance, and Shenstone knew that he had many causes of gratitude to
the Lytteltons. At least they deserve the praise
accorded to them by Graves, of discerning the poet's
merits beneath his bashfulness.

Of his literary achievements there is little that
need be said. The poetry, apart from *The Schoolmistress*, does not, for all the polishing it received,
stand out from the conventional mass of polite verse
which the century produced with so much—too much
—ease. The *Pastoral Ballad* and a handful of the
songs have considerable charm, but it is a charm
which can be discovered by the simple process of
reading them, and needs no comment. The elegies,
which precede Gray's great poem, and are more
original than those of Hammond, have little to
recommend them apart from their simplicity and the
fact, as their author says, that their pastoral elements
were taken from a pastoral setting. The *Levities, or
Pieces of Humour* contain some lively buffoonery, as
well as the famous *Lines written at an Inn* which
affected Dr Johnson 'with great emotion', and
aroused the reflection that nothing yet contrived by
man so much conduced to happiness as a good tavern.

[118]

But here again, it is no disparagement to say that their merits can be easily discovered. It is in prose that Shenstone's developed sensitivity best displays itself—in the letters, and in the aphorisms of *Men and Manners*. His meditative penetration found its fittest medium in these forms, and his reputation will come, it is probable, to depend mainly on them. It is worth recalling that on an afternoon when Johnson was 'full of critical severity' and would allow Shenstone little power of intellect, he yet agreed that it was a pity that John Whistler had destroyed Shenstone's letters to his brother Anthony, 'for, said he, Shenstone's correspondence was an honour'. And the title of one subsection from *Men and Manners*— *Egotisms from my own Sensations*—is a strange gesture from the 1750's, while from time to time a remark like 'Indolence is a kind of centripetal force' will witness to an introspective penetration of uncommon subtlety.

The correspondence, of course, reflects the private side of Shenstone's life, and sometimes suggests a man succumbing in a struggle for happiness too severe for his limited powers. When Columella satirizes his neighbour Nonesuch as 'one of the unthinking multitude who jog on in the beaten track of life', the hearty common sense of Graves counters him: 'Why, faith, I think that is the best *taste*, and the best system of philosophy, which makes a man happy and satisfied with himself.' But such robustness was beyond Shenstone's power. The letters, however, are the products of solitude, when he habitually recoiled on himself. It is always possible to distort by selection, and Dodsley unwittingly did this when he published Shenstone's letters without including those to Lady Luxborough. Life was chequered with happiness and misery, sickness and health, but these opposites held a fair proportion. 'Poor Shenstone, I am afraid he died of misery', said Johnson, who, thinking of the vanity of human wishes, found it affecting to consider how near he came to receiving the pension which would have relieved his difficulties. (A negotiation with Lord Bute to procure him £300 a year was proceeding successfully in January 1763. Shenstone died on 11 February.) But, in fact, the last letter which survives, of 16 January, far from dying of misery, proposes a visit to Lord Ward and declares that, the writer, being kept indoors by the frost, is 'quite pampered with Snipes & Fieldfare'. The Leasowes provided him with frequent periods of complacency, even of gleeful satisfaction, when he writes with a combination of excitement and playful exaggeration which recalls Walpole. Despite his premature feeling of age, he takes a joyful delight in 1762 at the behaviour of his principal cascade, which 'well resembles the playfulness of infancy; skipping from side to side, with a thousand antic motions, that answer no other purpose than the mere amusement of the proprietor'. In society, after the initial shyness wore off, he was a distinct success, and fulfilled the promise of his undergraduate days. The warm sun of admiration gratified him, and in its rays the

[120]

charm of his character expanded. A friend writing to Dodsley while the latter is visiting The Leasowes in 1759 congratulates him on being 'in Possession of a Happiness too great for Mortals; enjoying in one of the hottest Seasons that ever was known in *England*, the Shade and Coolness of the finest Groves perhaps in the World, rendered still more enchanting by the Conversation of one of the best Poets, as well as one of the worthiest Men of the Age.' Such tributes, obviously sincere, are frequent in contemporary references, apart from those of a small number who had no means of understanding him. The best expression of the place which he won in his friends' esteem occurs in a letter of 28 February 1763, from Percy to Grainger in the West Indies: 'I steal an hour from midnight to send you articles of intelligence.... It is the Death of our most elegant and amiable friend, Shenstone.... I know not any private gentleman whose loss has occasioned a more sincere or more universal concern. The delicate sensibility of his writings, the consummate elegance of his taste, the beauties of his conversation, and the virtues of his heart, had procured him a most extensive acquaintance, and every one of these aspired to his friendship, so that I know not an Instance of an event of this kind more deeply or more generally lamented.'

It would be unwise to claim for Shenstone a definitive influence in any direction. His originality anticipated, rather than revolutionized. The infiltration of Romanticism in England was extremely gradual, in comparison with its violent emergence in

France and Germany. It is not very helpful to class Shenstone as a pre-Romantic. Men do not need to be 'classed'. But for a label, it is near the truth to accept the epithet which Saintsbury applied to his verse—'the artificial-natural'. An American scholar, examining Dodsley's *Collection*, concludes quite fairly that 'the literature of the mid-eighteenth century is more hesitant and conservative, and has even less distinctive character, than is generally conceived' (R. D. Havens, *Changing Taste in the Eighteenth Century*; publications of the Modern Language Association of America, XLIV). This is a wise caution in all spheres of the century's life. There was a very long hesitation between the neo-classic discipline, with its weight of authority, and the new individualism. That Shenstone wrote of his own jasmines and harebells does not prove that he was nearer to Wordsworth than to Horace, or perhaps Virgil. That his friends thought of The Leasowes as 'Gothic'—which it was not—does not ally him with Romance rather than with Reason. That he chose his fashions to suit himself does not remove him from the heart of the eighteenth century.

It should be possible to define the character of the middle century pretty closely. To provide a full definition, unfortunately, the landscape must be viewed from a mountain of mediocrity which no one should have to climb. But a tentative definition might say that classicism and romanticism—whatever those terms mean—have generally been put on a see-saw. When they are up, they are up; and when

[122]

they are down, they are down. The point at which they are neither up nor down, though by its nature a transitional one, has at least a sort of equilibrium. The ascending and descending extremes are symmetrical about it.

To define a middle point is perhaps no more unsatisfactory than to define extremes. We should see the mid-century for what it was, rather than for what it was becoming—at least occasionally, lest we fall into the mistake that Pope made about women, that it has no character. It preserved the decorums. Its architecture was placid, or if it moved, as at Strawberry Hill, it unconsciously adapted its gait to the footsteps of tradition. Its gardening shook off an importation never very deeply rooted. Its church was, like the hermit in *Rasselas*, 'cheerful without levity, and pious without enthusiasm'. Books existed to teach the art of living, which it learned very well from the classics—'all ancient authors, Sir, all manly!' It greeted innovators with surprise—Shenstone's hair, Hanway's umbrella, Gray's *Odes*, Montgolfier's balloon. It grew, slowly, to respect the ladies. It discovered a divine approbation for commerce. It acquired one empire and lost another without so much as ruffling the tranquillity of its rural somnolence. Its 'characters' were legion—Parson Woodforde, who, every year, fired off his blunderbuss and gave three cheers by himself, to celebrate the Queen's birthday; squires who—*optimi corruptio pessima*—interpreted the picturesque for themselves; Beau Nash, whom Shenstone once saw

[123]

in his famous white hat, mild English counterpart of the continental adventurers like King Theodore and Casanova; Robert Bakewell, the farmer who entertained royalty in his kitchen; and scores of curious individuals who helped to gain the English a reputation for universal eccentricity, which at the same time was an eccentricity merely of personal habit, and not the deeper originality of individual thought. It half-blunderingly created its greatest poem, the pastoral landscape of England. 'It is still by no means realized', Professor Patrick Abercrombie has written, 'how much of England was consciously laid out during this time, far beyond the boundary of the home park. For example, in the Thames Valley, in the neighbourhood of the Goring Gap, the downs were nearly bare of verdure 150 years ago: there is evidence here of the careful work of landscape planting, which gives its characteristic appearance to this beautiful stretch of river.... The regularizing and angular hand of man has thus been softened into heightening an effect here, opening a prospect there, or planting out an unseemly object.' In spirit it could mellow into the leisureliness of Gibbon, could retreat from the towns to the country-side under the impact of industrialism, and read Horace in its vicarages, where, in fact, it may still occasionally be found.

Such a list has no limits. It does not finally *prove* anything. But it is useful to remember the sort of things which the century produced, and which constitute its character. Above all, it found its chief concern in social relations, and it lived with its feet on the ground, wherever its head happened temporarily to be.

As for The Leasowes, its brief hour faded with the age that gave it birth. For several years it was an object of interest. Johnson visited it on 19 September 1774, and despite continual rain inspected all the waterfalls, at least with sufficient care to notice that in one place there were 'fourteen falls in a short line'. Wesley saw it in 1782 and wrote: 'I doubt if it be exceeded by anything in Europe.' But its eventual fate, as Goldsmith remarked, is 'a true picture of sublunary vicissitude'. Shenstone's revulsion from 'the vulgar' was partly due, it will be remembered, to the freedoms which the vulgar sometimes took with his flowers. Delicately appealing as it did to a cultivated taste, The Leasowes was caviare to the general. The result, according to Goldsmith, was that 'all the windows of his temples and the walls of his retreats were impressed with the characters of ignorance, profaneness, and obscenity, and his lawns worn bare'. The violence of the well-intentioned Wildgoose was a trifle light as air compared with the playful iconoclasm of sight-seers. The obelisks did not always stand up under the trials of strength to which they were subjected; the urns were set rolling down the hillsides; and the seats disappeared for firewood. Even the better-behaved were perhaps as insensitive as the visitor who commented: 'A sweet, snug, little farm—what a pity it is so hilly, and so overrun with trees' (*Blackwood's Edinburgh Maga-*

zine, 1823). 'Eventually, the ruinated Priory wall became too thoroughly a ruin, and the punch-bowl was shivered on its stand.' The value of the estate rose steeply, from just over £3000 to £17,000 in fifteen years; but the timber came down, and the house was rebuilt. A more enterprising generation than Shenstone's has dammed his valley with a railway embankment, filled the middle distance with slate roofs and factory chimneys, and adorned the prospect with an enamelled advertisement for steel in large white letters. Elegance is out-of-date; we cannot afford good taste.

So there are no signs that The Leasowes dramatically affected the course of appreciation. It had little of the *éclat* of Strawberry Hill. Its owner differed remarkably from the cosmopolitan Walpole. Its sincerity and charm are mentioned with respect by subsequent historians of landscape, but its slightly specialized appeal, its economy of means and good-mannered lack of pretence, prevented any dynamic movement from springing from it. It remains, therefore, as a kind of definition of what its generation, at its most cultured, was. It confirms an impression of mental order which did not mean a lack of deep feeling, a decorous exterior not due solely to complacency, a search for variety and personal expression which still would not break too violently with the past. 'A place of rest and refreshment'—it typifies its age in that. 'The artificial-natural'—in that too. There is nothing doctrinaire about it. It appeals to the pillars of the Established

Church. Its inscriptions quote Ovid, Virgil, Horace, and Pope. It is a foot-hill to Parnassus where the average poets of the time, their wings too weak to fly to the mountain itself, can comfortably cluster. It links itself to the new-found popularity of the ballads and of Spenser. In its concern with obelisks and cascades it sees but scarcely excites itself over the '45 and the *annus mirabilis* of '59. The shadow of the dark satanic mills was already falling on the Yorkshire valleys during the later years of its life, Brindley was digging the Duke of Bridgewater's canal from Worsley to Manchester, and stage-coaches made the journey from London to Bath in a day. But this was far removed from its ken. A bend in a walk, or the disposition of an urn, the orientation of a vista or the meandering of a stream, were the graces it assumed to attract the attentions of the cultured; and its owner, far from the bustle of the busy town, cultivated a sociable conversation and an elegant muse for the delight of himself and his friends, perhaps guessing but hardly caring that the noise of greater movements would shortly obliterate the gossip of his little circle. There is no better epitaph for him than those few lines of Horace which he chose to inscribe on one of his urns:

> mihi parva rura et
> Spiritum Graiæ tenuem camenæ
> Parca non mendax dedit, et malignum
> Spernere vulgus.

[127]

APPENDIX

THE DATING OF SHENSTONE'S LETTERS

The dates given to the letters printed in Shenstone's *Collected Works* in 1769 were in many cases supplied by Robert Dodsley, and the earlier ones are frequently inaccurate. The evidence has been closely sifted by John Edwin Wells (*The Dating of Shenstone's Letters*; in *Anglia*, Band xxxv, 1911–12, p. 429), and James F. Fullington (*The Dating of Shenstone's Letters*; in the publications of the Modern Language Association of America, Volume xlvi, 1931, p. 1128). I have accepted their conclusions, and when referring to the date of a letter have, whenever necessary, amended Dodsley's date according to the following table. The corrections are those of Wells, unless otherwise attributed. I have ignored the instances where the evidence is merely corroborative.

Letter	Date in *Works*, 1769	Correction
I	1739	
II	22 July 1739	22 July 1741
III	1739	Between 29 Sept. and 24 Oct. 1740
IV	1739	Shortly after 13 Feb. 1741
V	6 Feb. 1740	6 Feb. 1741
VI	30 Apr. 1740	30 Apr. 1741
VII	28 Aug. 1740	28 Aug. 1741
VIII	Aug. 1740	
IX	1740	16–17 Jan. 1741
X	1740, 'March, Tuesday night'	9 Mar. 1742

Letter	Date in *Works*, 1769	Correction
XI	1740	Probably autumn 1740
XII	21 Jan. 1741	
XIII	1741	Probably after March 1742
XIV	8 June 1741	8 June 1741 or 1742
XV	23 Sept. 1741	
XVI	1741	
XVII	1741	June 1742
XVIII	17 June 1741	
XIX	25 Nov. 1741	
XX	1741	Probably 1742
XXI	(wrongly numbered XXII) 1741	Just after 19 July 1742
XXII	19 Jan. 1741/2	
XXIII	1742. 'The Day before Christmas'	24 Dec. 1741
XXIV	June 1742	
XXV	No date	Probably 17–18 May 1742
XXVI	Nov. 1742	
XXVII	About 1743	Late Feb. 1742
XXVIII	16 Feb. 1743	
XXIX	1743	Not later than Aug. 1742
XXX	1743	30 May 1744
XXXI	1743	After 9 July 1743. [Fullington: 'about the middle of Aug. 1743']
XXXII	No date	About July 1743. [Fullington: 'shortly after 9 or 16 July 1743']
XXXIII	9 July 1743	
XXXIV	3 July 1743	
XXXV	9 Nov. 1743	
XXXVI	23 Dec. 1743	
XXXVII	1743	
XXXVIII	1 Mar. 1743/4	
XXXIX	About 1745	[Fullington: late 1744 or 1745]
XL	22 Nov. 1745	
XLI	1746 'ineunte anno'	After 18 Aug. 1746
XLII	6 Apr. 1746	
XLIII	11 May 1746	

Letter	Date in *Works*, 1769	Correction
XLIV	'June the last, 1747'	Probably 1748
XLV	21 Sept. 1747	
XLVI	1747	[Fullington: 1743 or 1744]
XLVII	'about the 20th of Sept. 1747'	
XLVIII	1747	Shortly before No. XLIX
XLIX	14 Feb. 1747/8	
L	23 Mar. 1747/8	
LI	'written August 21, 1748'	
LII	3 Sept. 1748	
LIII	11 Sept. 1748	
LIV	13 Nov.	After 11 Sept. 1748
LV	June 1749	25 or 26 June 1749
LVI	June 1749	[Fullington: about 1 June 1749]
LVII	9 July 1749	
LVIII	15 Mar. 1749/50	
LIX	11 June 1750	
LX	9 Sept. 1750	
LXI	2 Nov. 1750	
LXII	No date	Very soon after 24 Mar. 1748

All the letters after No. LXII appear to be correctly dated with the exception of

XC	About 1757	[Fullington: between 5 Jan. and 23 Mar. 1758]

INDEX

[133]

LaVergne, TN USA
05 December 2009
166031LV00007BA/1/P

9 780521 125277

Paperback Re-issue

First published in 1937, by Arthur Raleigh Humphreys, this four-part volume traces the life of the English poet William Shenstone (1714-1763) from his birth in Halesowen, Shropshire to his death at the famous estate, The Leasowes. Through a detailed examination of Shenstone's poetical works and personal correspondence, Professor Humphreys assembles a vivid sketch of his life and character while also setting right some of the damages of neglect done to his literary legacy. This work remains one of the few reliable studies of a poet on whom too little scholarship exists.

CAMBRIDGE
UNIVERSITY PRESS
www.cambridge.org

ISBN 978-0-521-12527-